A Gift of the
Orinda Junior Women's Club

Tales and Treasures
of
CALIFORNIA'S
RANCHOS

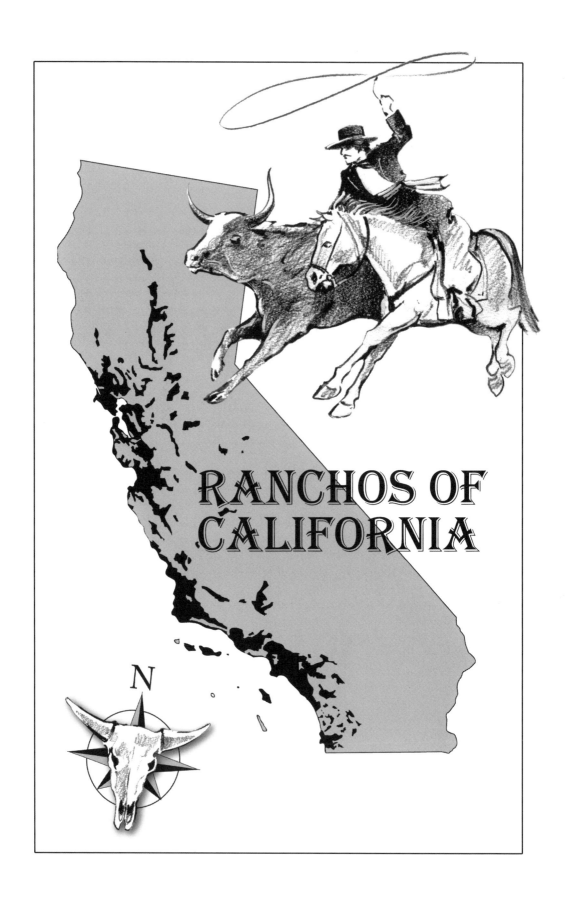

RANCHOS OF CALIFORNIA

N

Tales and Treasures

of

CALIFORNIA'S RANCHOS

Randall A. Reinstedt

Illustrated by Ed Greco

Ghost Town Publications

Randall A. Reinstedt's
History & Happenings of California Series
Ghost Town Publications
P.O. Drawer 5998
Carmel, CA 93921

Manufactured in the United States of America

10 9 8 7 6 5 4 3 2 1

Library of Congress Catalog Number 98-070085
ISBN 0-933818-29-7 Hardcover
ISBN 0-933818-82-3 Softcover

Edited by John Bergez
Cover design and illustrations by Ed Greco
Interior design and typesetting by Erick and Mary Ann Reinstedt

CONTENTS

PART ONE

RANCHO DAYS

1  A GOLDEN AGE?

This book is about the special places known as California ranchos. The word *rancho* is Spanish and means a ranch or, if you like, a farm where animals and crops were raised. California's ranchos were land holdings that were granted to individuals during the time when Spanish-speaking people ruled California. Often these grants of land were very sizable, and some of the owners (called *rancheros*, or ranchers) became quite wealthy.

I'll tell you more about the days of the Spanish and Mexican ranchos in a moment. First, though, you might be wondering why the title of this book talks about "tales and treasures" of California's ranchos. Well, those grants of land covered a lot of territory, often in places that were very desirable to live in. Over the years, the happenings in and around these prized properties gave rise to many fascinating stories. Quite a few of these tales concern treasures of various kinds.

Now, the word "treasure" means different things to different people. You will read about many kinds of treasures in Part Two of this book. Among them are a priceless collection of ancient bones, hoards of money and valuable objects, rich deposits of gold and other minerals, the buried bandit loot of a famous outlaw, and a fabulous castle full of one-of-a-kind objects from around the world. These treasures and many more, along with countless tales of colorful characters from the past, are all part of the story of California's ranchos.

To me, though, another kind of "treasure" is the memory of the way things used to be. Knowing about the past makes our everyday surroundings even more special, especially for those of us who are lucky enough to live in

California. Our heritage includes everything from prehistoric animals to California Indians, Spanish explorers and padres, Russian trappers, Mexican and Spanish rancheros, American settlers and soldiers, rough-and-ready gold seekers, and millions of men and women from around the world who have come to the Golden State dreaming of a better life. It would be hard to name a place that has a richer or more colorful past. And it is this fascinating history that makes California what it is today.

An important part of this history is the period that I refer to as "rancho days." To some people, these years were a time of sadness and hardship, while to others they were a "Golden Age" of happy times. As you learn more about this period in this chapter and the next one, perhaps you'll agree with me that rancho days were a little bit of both.

The story of California's ranchos begins in the late 1700s, when the government of Spain began to let former soldiers use large areas of land for ranching or farming. But when most people think of rancho days, they think of the years when California was under Mexican rule, especially the 1830s and early to mid-1840s. It was then that most of the ranchos were established and the rancheros and their families enjoyed their happiest times.

Mexico gained its independence from Spain and took control of Alta (Upper) California in the early 1820s. By the 1830s, the Mexican government was changing some of the ways the Spanish had done things. In particular, Mexico's new leaders disliked the way the old Spanish missions were being run. They decided that the missions would have to give up much of their land. In time this meant that thousands of acres of prize property would be freed up.

Half of the land was supposed to go to the mission Indians, who had worked it for so many years. Unfortunately for the Indians, it didn't always work out that way. Instead, much of the property ended up in the hands

of leading
families who were
already large landowners.
Sometimes grants were given as
a reward for service to the government
(or a particular governor), and sometimes
they were given to encourage settlers, including some
Americans.

As you might guess from the name "rancho," these
land grants were mostly used for raising cattle and other
animals. Most of the ranchos were located near the Pacific
coast, and much of rancho life centered on what was
known as the "hide and tallow trade." The rancheros used
their animals to produce hides (skins) and tallow (fat),
which they traded for goods brought to the coast by ships.
(Tallow was used for making such things as soap and
candles. The "tallow trade" was not as important as the
trading of hides.)

Many of the trade vessels that brought goods to
California came from the Atlantic coast side of our
continent. They were often called "Boston traders" or
"Boston ships" because many of them sailed from the
harbor of Boston, Massachusetts. They got to California
by sailing all the way around the tip of South America.
Packed aboard these vessels were the kinds of things that
were needed and wanted by the *Californios* (Spanish-
speaking Californians).

11

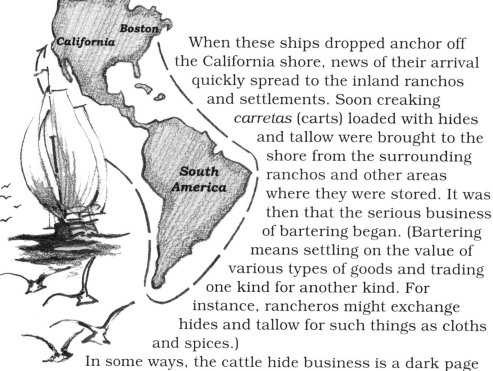

When these ships dropped anchor off the California shore, news of their arrival quickly spread to the inland ranchos and settlements. Soon creaking *carretas* (carts) loaded with hides and tallow were brought to the shore from the surrounding ranchos and other areas where they were stored. It was then that the serious business of bartering began. (Bartering means settling on the value of various types of goods and trading one kind for another kind. For instance, rancheros might exchange hides and tallow for such things as cloths and spices.)

In some ways, the cattle hide business is a dark page in California history. Thousands of animals were cruelly killed for their skins. Sometimes part of the meat was cut and dried so that it could be eaten later, while the fat was cooked and made into tallow. All too often, though, the skinned carcasses (bodies) were simply left in the fields to rot or to be eaten by wild animals.

Reports from this time describe California's hills and valleys as "dotted" with the decaying bodies of cattle. One grisly account comes from an artist who visited the area in 1841. He remembered traveling at night on horseback and being struck by the eerie sound of the "bleached and brittle" bones of dead cattle being crushed by the hoofs of his horse as he rode along.

If you're like me, you're probably glad that such gruesome sounds and sights are no longer part of the California scene. In other ways, though, rancho families enjoyed a life that seems pleasant even today. It must have been a thrill for them to visit the incoming vessels and explore their cargoes. Except for a few simple household crafts, Californians of that period depended almost entirely on trade vessels to supply their needs. You might say that, to them, the ships were floating shopping malls!

What kinds of goods did the Boston traders carry in their holds? To give you an idea, here is a description

written by a man who was on board the ship *Pilgrim* when it called at Monterey in 1835:

> Our cargo was an assorted one; that is, it consisted of everything under the sun. We had spirits [liquors] of all kinds . . . , teas, coffee, sugar, spices, raisins, molasses, hardware, crockery-ware, tin-ware, cutlery, clothing of all kinds, boots and shoes from Lynn, calicoes and cottons from Lowell, crapes, silks; also, shawls, scarfs, necklaces, jewelry, and combs for the women; furniture; and, in fact, everything that can be imagined, from Chinese fireworks to English cartwheels—of which we had a dozen pairs with their iron tires on.

This list is certainly impressive. I might add that vessels of this kind were also known to carry such sizable items as billiard tables and pianos!

Like other visitors to California, the trade ship captains often were amazed at how big many of the ranchos were. In fact, many of these privately owned properties stretched for many miles in all directions. To take just one example, an 1820 grant established a rancho along the east shore of San Francisco Bay. This property took in all the land occupied by the present-day cities of Alameda, Oakland, and Berkeley—and that was only *part* of this large grant!

As big as this bayside property was, there were other ranchos that were more than twice its size. For instance, one southern California rancho (near present-day Los Angeles) consisted of more than 100,000 acres, or more than 150 square miles! (If you want to get an idea of how big this is, try drawing a box on a map of California. Using the "miles" scale on the map, make each side of the box equal to 150 miles. That's how much territory belonged to this one ranchero. Pretty impressive, isn't it?)

The main house of this property contained more than 45 rooms, and 26 servants helped to keep its occupants happy. The owner of this rancho also employed more than 100 *vaqueros* (cowboys). Others who worked on the property were skilled in such trades as carpentry, leather tanning, shoemaking, plastering, harness making, wool combing, and wine making. A dairyman was also on the staff. His duties included milking cows and making butter and cheese.

Even this number of workers was small compared to the number that some of the other land owners employed. As just one example, Mariano Vallejo oversaw approximately 600 vaqueros (and assorted other workers) who helped maintain his holdings in present-day Sonoma and Solano counties.

These gigantic ranchos dwarfed many others that were much smaller. But even though owning more land or more cattle might make a ranchero "richer" in one way, sometimes it could be like having money you can't spend.

Cattle were useful mostly for providing the hides and tallow that could be bartered for goods aboard the trade ships. There were only so many things a ranchero could "buy" in this way, and there were only so many ships that came to California each year. So simply owning more heads of cattle didn't always make a ranchero that much better off than his neighbor.

In fact, some *Californios* felt they were "wealthier" if they had a small rancho in a good location, combined with a "workable" number of cattle. After all, less land and fewer heads of cattle meant less work and fewer worries—and more time to enjoy life.

As we'll talk about more in the next chapter, enjoying life was something that these early Californians prized. They built comfortable homes and enjoyed sharing them with travelers and friends. There was very little crime during this time, with things like theft and murder being quite rare. Land was plentiful, the country was beautiful, and the hustle and bustle of great cities were still in the future. To many landowners and their families, rancho days truly were a Golden Age.

To others, though, the coming of the ranchos brought heartache and hard times. Certainly this was true of many of the native people of California, whose way of life had already changed with the arrival of the Spanish years before. Things didn't get much better for these California Indians during the rancho period, especially those who were used to the mission way of life.

As I mentioned earlier, much of the mission land was supposed to be given to the Indians who had worked the property. Instead, it often ended up in the hands of others. As a result, many of the Indians began living and working on the ranchos. Although they were given food and clothing, they received little pay, and sometimes none at all. A number of the men became vaqueros, and before long they were known for being among the most expert horseback riders in the world. But even if they enjoyed what they were doing at times, they had many reasons to be unhappy with the way things had turned out.

Even for the fortunate landowners, though, the Golden Age would come to an end all too soon. While some of the ranchos survived for a number of years, the American conquest of California in 1846 was the beginning of the end of rancho days. As the new government was established and more and more settlers arrived, rancheros found themselves losing much of their land. Things only got worse a few years later, when hordes of fortune hunters overran parts of California during the Gold Rush. After that, life would never be quite the same.

Later in this book, you'll read more about what happened to some rancheros during the American conquest and the Gold Rush. First, though, let's take a closer look at what life was like on the ranchos during the years when Mexico still controlled Alta California. As you read the next chapter, try to picture yourself as a member of a ranchero's family, or as a great landowner yourself. Imagine telling your children and grandchildren what rancho days were like. Do you think you would describe them as . . . *a Golden Age?*

LIFE ON THE RANCHOS

What was it like to live on a California rancho? As I mentioned in Chapter 1, during rancho days much of people's lives revolved around the business of raising cattle for the hide and tallow trade. For many Californians, cattle were the main source of wealth, trade, food, and work.

Although raising cattle can be hard work, life on the ranchos was peaceful and unhurried compared to the way most people live today. At least, that was true for the landowners who could afford to hire large numbers of workers to help manage the cattle, maintain the ranch buildings, tend crops, and perform other chores. These lucky rancheros were quite happy with their way of life, and many of them enjoyed sharing their good fortune with friends and strangers alike.

Today most Californians live in and around towns and cities. These busy places are where most of us work, shop, go to school, and look for entertainment. Rancheros, however, lived in homes that were widely scattered, and most of their work and play took place right on the rancho itself. Travelers, too, had few places to turn when they needed a place to stay, a change of horses, or something to eat. So it's little wonder that a ranchero's home was often a hotel, restaurant, and social gathering place, all rolled into one.

As with many of the buildings in California at this time, the rancheros' houses were usually made out of sun-dried adobe bricks. These bricks were made from a mixture of clay-like soil, water, and weeds. The walls of

these dwellings were often quite thick, which helped to keep them cool in the summer and warm in the winter.

The structures were frequently built around a patio. It was here that family members spent much of their time. The patios were also used for special gatherings and to entertain guests.

Speaking of guests, history books tell of many rancheros who opened their houses and lands to all who passed by. Visitors to California could travel from rancho to rancho without fear of being turned away. Not only were they warmly welcomed, but often they were free to stay as long as they wished. When it was time for them to leave, they might find a fresh horse saddled and waiting—as well as coins left in their rooms to help them on their way!

Such accounts of a "Golden Age" of pleasant and generous living may be a little exaggerated. Still, most history buffs seem to agree that life was good to the rancheros. And if a neighbor was in need, the rancheros shared what they had without thought of being repaid.

Respect and trust were also important within families. Most rancheros were dedicated fathers and husbands. The children, too, are said to have had great respect for their parents.

Rancheros' families, by the way, were often quite large. Families with six or more children were common, and it wasn't unusual to see more than twice that number! And that's only part of the story. When the children grew up and had families of their own, things really began to get interesting. To take just one example, a well-known member of the Pico clan lived to the age of 74. When he died, he left 15 children, 116 grandchildren, and 97 great-grandchildren!

Even though a ranchero might have a lot of children, not all of them went to school. Schools were few and far between during this time. Even when there was a school to go to, usually it was only the boys who were allowed to attend. Girls were taught at home, where they learned such crafts as cooking and sewing.

Maybe the girls were lucky, because schoolboys in old California didn't have it easy. Many of the early teachers were former soldiers, and most of them were quite strict. When one of their students didn't learn his lessons, he was often punished with a whip!

Because many of the early schools were not very good, some rancheros chose other ways of providing education for their sons. Some hired their own teachers. Others sent their boys away to school in such faraway places as Hawaii, Boston, and Valparaiso (in the South American country of Chile).

For those family members who stayed at home, a high-light of rancho life was the arrival of a trading vessel. Visits aboard these vessels were more than just occasions for doing business. Rancheros and their families also looked forward to them as social events. When the bartering was over,

many of the ship's officers were invited to the homes of those who lived in the area. The visitors brought news as well as a bit of excitement to their hosts. In turn, they enjoyed the friendliness of the people and eagerly awaited their trips ashore.

Many activities added to the fun of these visits. Wealthy *Californios* needed little reason to host a party or take part in picnics, receptions in honor of visiting guests, and fiestas that could last for several days.

Of course, not everyone was as fortunate as the well-to-do rancheros and their families. Life was harder for the workers on the ranchos, especially those California Indians who received only food, clothing, and shelter in return for their labor. But the workers, too, sometimes got to share in fun events.

Among these activities were the *rodeos* (roundups) that were held each year, usually in the spring. The rodeos weren't just about having fun. They were also important in helping the ranchos to run effectively. In those days California's vast open ranges didn't have fences, so cattle could roam freely. The roundups were needed so that vaqueros from neighboring ranchos could work together to gather the animals and herd them to the rodeo site.

When the cattle were gathered at one of the ranchos, they were sorted out by the brands in their hides. Then unbranded calves were singled out and branded with their home brand. In this way a ranchero and his *mayordomo* (manager) could get an idea of the size of their herd and the number of cattle they could profitably kill during the coming season.

The roundups usually lasted for several days, and sometimes as long as a week. Often the families of the rancheros and their vaqueros gathered at the site. While the men worked with the cattle during the day, the women sewed, sang, and visited with one another. The children, too, enjoyed their time together as they played, picnicked, and watched the men brand the cattle.

When darkness fell and the day's work was done, the real fun began. Guitars were brought out, food was served, and the people sang, danced, and enjoyed one another's company. No matter how tiring the day's work had been, the festivities often lasted far into the night.

The biggest party of all was held when the branding was over. It was then that a huge feast was served and special games were played. The men showed off their riding skills by performing tricks and competing in races and games in front of enthusiastic spectators who clapped and shouted and cheered them on.

One of the most popular and difficult of the games involved a rooster. The unhappy bird was buried up to its neck in the ground (or in the sand, if the game was played on the beach), so that only its head was showing. When the rooster was firmly planted, a signal was sent to a rider waiting on horseback about 200 feet away. Upon getting the signal, he spurred his mount toward the bird. Charging down the straightaway as fast as he could ride, the horseman would lean over as far as he dared and attempt to grab the creature by the head and yank it from the ground.

As you can imagine, this game was both dangerous and exciting. It took a great deal of skill for a rider to lean down from a galloping horse, pluck a rooster from the ground, right himself in the saddle, and wave the wing-flapping bird in the air—all while riding at top speed! Those who succeeded in grabbing the rooster won whoops of admiration from the spectators.

Incidentally, it wasn't only the men who were good with horses. The motto of these early Californians seemed to be "Why walk when you can ride?" Young boys often began their horseback-riding careers at the age of four or five. Women and girls frequently became expert riders, too.

As I mentioned a moment ago, the yearly rodeos helped rancheros to keep track of their huge herds of cattle. Even so, it was impossible to control the animals completely or even to know exactly how many were roaming the ranges. As time went on, and the cattle continued to multiply, a number of problems arose.

One problem was the wildness of the animals. It seems that the freedom to roam also brought a "free spirit" to some of these creatures, making them quite ferocious. As a result, anyone who ventured out among the herds had to be armed and on horseback.

The bulls, in particular, had to be watched. They were often compared to the California grizzly bear for their

savagery. Frequently vaqueros sought out especially ferocious bulls and brought them to nearby ranchos or settlements. There they pitted the bulls against equally fierce grizzlies in bull-and-bear fights. Sad to say, these bloody events were popular pastimes, and people came from miles around to watch these bold creatures battle to the death.

Problems on the pastures also arose during dry years, when lack of rain meant that the grasslands could not produce enough food for the animals. At such times vaqueros were forced to weed out the cattle by killing the older animals so that the others would have enough food.

Too many horses could create similar problems. As a result, many fine animals were sacrificed, especially mares (females) that might produce still more young. A number of horses met their end at the bottom of a cliff, having been driven over the edge by a team of vaqueros.

As sad as such things seem, they were a part of rancho life. Perhaps even more cruel was the gathering of "California bank notes." This nickname was given to dried cowhides because they were used in place of money to purchase or barter for goods. As I described in the first chapter, often cattle were skinned for their hides and their bodies left to rot or to be eaten by other animals.

Rather than end this chapter on that sad note, let me go back to one of the more pleasant parts of rancho life. As California's population grew, so did the number of social gatherings. In addition to the rodeos, festivities of other kinds also were popular. Among them was the fandango, or dance party. Many early Californians were excellent dancers, and they greatly enjoyed these evening gatherings. Sometimes they danced until morning!

One of the most popular dances in the capital community of Monterey (as well as other locations) was the *cascarón* ball. To make the *cascarone*, a hole was carefully made in the end of an egg. After the insides were removed, the shell was filled with tiny pieces of colored paper. Sometimes other things were added, such as perfumed water. The egg was then sealed with wax. At the dances the *cascarones* were broken over the heads of the dancers, adding fun and excitement to the gatherings.

Fandangos, fiestas, rodeos, visits from Boston traders—all these colorful events added to the special lifestyle that the rancheros and their families enjoyed. Along with the *Californios'* famous hospitality and generosity to friends and strangers alike, these festive occasions helped to make rancho days a golden time for many landowners and their families.

All too soon, however, a number of changes combined to bring an end to rancho days. In 1846, peaceful times gave way to war between the United States and Mexico, with Alta California being part of the prize that went to the victorious Americans. With a new government in control, some holders of land grants found it hard to hang on to all the property they believed was theirs.

Things changed even more after gold was discovered in the Sierra Nevada in 1848. As gold seekers began to overrun California, some of the large landowners began looking at their huge herds of cattle in a new light. With thousands of miners combing the western slope of the Sierras, there wasn't enough food to go around. That gave the rancheros the idea of "striking it rich" their own way. Herding their cattle, they drove them to the Gold Country, where they could be sold for high prices.

In time the gold became harder to find, and many of the miners began drifting away from the Sierras. As they made their way to other areas, they became impressed with the land and the open spaces they saw around them. Many of these frustrated fortune hunters had been farmers before striking out for the gold fields, and they knew good land when they saw it. Naturally enough, they decided to settle down. Often the place they decided to call "home" was rancho land.

It wasn't easy for the rancheros to defend their land claims. Sometimes they weren't sure themselves exactly where their property began and ended. In addition, questions were raised about a number of grants that were given during the last few months of Mexican rule. It was left to a specially formed United States Land Commission, along with American courts, to try to settle arguments about who owned which land. Often enough the rancheros wound up on the losing side.

To some, the gold discovery and the arrival of thousands of newcomers spelled the beginning of the end for rancho days. Others believe that the rancheros' way of life was doomed once the United States took over the territory from Mexico.

Still others think that the final blow came during the 1860s, when a severe drought hit the Golden State. During this time thousands of cattle died, and many rancheros lost what was left of their fortunes and their land. Even so, some of the great cattle-bearing ranchos did manage to last into the 1900s.

Today, the rancho period lives only in memory, and in the many stories that have sprung up around the sites of the great land grants. In the rest of this book, you will read about tales and treasures that are connected with many of these locations. As you do, I think you will agree with me that knowing about the heritage of California's ranchos makes living in the Golden State that much more special!

PART TWO

RANCHO TALES AND TREASURES

RANCHO LA BREA

R ancho La Brea is located in Los Angeles
County. It was first granted to Antonio Jose
Rocha and Nemicio Dominguez in 1828. The
original grant was for approximately 4,439 acres.
The rancho gained its name from *brea* (a tar-like
substance) that seeped from the ground.

Too Many Treasures to Count

I'd like to start this collection of tales and treasures with a
story about a very special rancho in southern California.
One reason this rancho is special is that one of the largest
cities in the United States grew up around it. But what
really makes this rancho different is the "treasure" it is
best known for. In the opinion of many modern-day
scientists, the value of this treasure is so great that it
can't be measured in money!

If you live in or near the city of Los Angeles, you may
already know about the fabulous finds that have been
made on this land. However, I wonder how many people
are aware of the ancient and priceless items that are *still*
being found there.

This mysterious wealth is not gold or silver, or any of
the other more common kinds of riches that Nature has
hidden in its vast treasure chest. Instead, this rancho's
treasure consists of the thousands of *fossils* that have

been recovered on its grounds. (A fossil is the preserved remains of a living thing such as a plant or animal.)

The most famous of the fossils are bones from beasts that are now *extinct* (no longer living anywhere on Earth). These fossilized bones have been found in a variety of shapes and sizes, from the smallest of rodents to the huge imperial mammoth (the largest member of the elephant family ever found in North America). Countless other kinds of fossil remains have also been recovered from the site. The collection includes such things as seeds, wood, leaves, insects, spiders, snails, frogs, toads, turtles, snakes, and birds.

Why have so many fossils been found in this particular spot? The answer to this question also explains how this rancho got its name. You see, Rancho La Brea means "the tar ranch." The name was given to the rancho in honor of the black goo that oozed from the ground in certain areas of the property. The Spanish called the sticky stuff *brea* (tar). And it is the tar that is the secret to the rancho's treasure trove of fossils.

In days of old, probably long before human beings came to southern California, countless animals roamed the region. Usually they avoided the sticky tar. Sometimes, though, they got stuck in the stuff. Perhaps this would happen after a rainstorm, when water settled on top of the tar. At such times animals may have waded into the water to get a drink, only to find themselves "glued" to the tar underneath. If something like this did take place, it is easy to imagine other animals

coming along and sensing an easy kill. Then they might have attacked the helpless creatures—and become stuck themselves!

You can probably think of more ways in which animals (and other things such as leaves or seeds) might have become trapped in the tar. Now imagine such happenings taking place over a very long time, perhaps many thousands of years. You can easily see how countless forms of life could have become mired in the goo. In time their remains turned to fossils.

The first people who came upon La Brea's tar were California Indians. Long before men from other lands arrived, the Indians were aware of the sticky stuff. They used it for many different purposes, such as making their baskets watertight and waterproofing their boats. In 1769, when Spanish explorers came to the area, they too found the tar. During the Mission Period, the padres and some of the Spanish settlers put the goop on their roofs to help keep the rain out.

The tar continued to be important during rancho days. In fact, it was so useful that it was protected by the original Rancho La Brea land grant of 1828. Even though the grant gave two men ownership of the land, it also gave local people permission to take as much *brea* from the property as they needed.

The pitch-like tar that many of these people used is also called asphalt. Along with the asphalt there was another gooey liquid. Today this liquid is refined and made into a number of products, including gasoline. It is so valuable that it has been called "black gold."

We know this liquid as oil. Like real gold, it is one of the Golden State's many natural treasures.

To me, though, the greatest riches connected with the La Brea "tar pits" are the fossils that are still being found there. These ancient remains are telling fascinating stories

about the plants and animals that lived in the Los Angeles area between 4,000 and 40,000 years ago.

I've already mentioned one of the interesting animals that once lived in southern California, the imperial mammoth. This hairy member of the elephant family grew to more than 13 feet in height and weighed more than 10,000 pounds (about the size of a modern-day African elephant). And did you know that there was a second beast that also boasted an elephant-like trunk? This creature was the American mastodon. It resembled the mammoth in having a trunk and shaggy hair, but it was smaller than its distant cousin and had more teeth.

There were also other sizable animals that roamed the area around La Brea in ancient times and got caught in the tar. Among them were the ground sloth, the short-faced bear, the western camel, the American lion, and the long-horned bison. This last creature was larger than the bison we know today. It isn't called "long-horned" for nothing. This impressive beast boasted a set of horns that measured six feet across!

My favorite La Brea creature is the saber-toothed cat (sometimes called the saber-toothed tiger). This animal was about the size of a modern-day African lion. It got its name from the shape of its two upper teeth, which were curved like sabers (a type of sword). These fang-like teeth were extremely sharp and grew to about eight inches in length! (Try measuring this length with a ruler. Pretty impressive, isn't it?) The scientific name of the saber-toothed cat is *Smilodon californicus*, and it is the official California state fossil. (Maybe that's why I like it so much.)

As you have probably guessed, the animals that I have just mentioned are all extinct. We know about them only because of fossils like the ones that have been found at La Brea. It's no wonder that this area has become famous for its fossilized bones and other ancient treasures.

It isn't only large animals that have left their mark in the La Brea tar pits. More than 100,000 plant fossils have also been recovered there. Insects and spiders (and their kin) boast big numbers, too. As with plants, the fossilized remains of over 100,000 such creatures have been found.

And then there are the birds! Did you know that the world's largest collection of fossilized birds has been taken from the La Brea deposits? Once again, over 100,000 specimens (fossil finds) have been recorded. They include examples of more than 135 different species of birds (19 of these species are extinct).

The largest extinct bird found at La Brea is known as Merriam's Teratorn. The remains of more than 100 of these huge creatures have been found. To get an idea of this bird's size, try laying 17 copies of this book (or one of similar size) end to end. A Teratorn could spread its wings and reach across all those books! In case you're wondering how this compares with modern-day birds, the Teratorn's wingspan of about 14 feet is longer than the wingspan of the California condor (the largest land bird in North America).

In all, more than one million separate fossils have been taken from the grounds of Rancho La Brea. That's quite a collection—especially when you consider the fact that people didn't start seriously collecting the fossils until the early 1900s! Now add in the tar that was so useful to the Indians and Spanish settlers, not to mention the "black gold" that has been pumped from the area. With all these things in mind, you can see how Rancho La Brea has earned its claim to fame.

Even today, lucky Los Angelenos, as well as visitors from far and wide, flock to the grounds of this former rancho. There they enjoy the modern-day treasure of a beautiful park, complete with a museum where they can see examples of many of La Brea's famous fossils.

So you see, this California rancho was, and continues to be, special for a number of reasons. And when it comes to riches, I think we can all agree that Rancho La Brea has *too many treasures to count!*

RANCHO NUESTRA SENORA DEL REFUGIO

Rancho Nuestra Senora del Refugio is located in Santa Barbara County. It was provisionally granted to Jose Francisco Ortega in the mid-1790s. The original grant was for approximately 26,529 acres. The name means Our Lady of the Refuge.

A Pirate Leaves More Than He Takes

In this chapter we move north from Los Angeles to a rancho in Santa Barbara County that has its own special claim to fame. This seaside property is the only California rancho that was ever attacked by a pirate!

The name of the dreaded sea captain was Hippolyte de Bouchard. Along with his band of buccaneers, this fiery Frenchman brought fear and destruction to the people who lived along the California coast. But, as we will see, in attacking a California rancho he also left something behind that proved to be more valuable than anything he took.

Strangely enough, the only rancho to suffer a pirate attack had a name that suggested a "safe place."

Officially, it was known as Nuestra Senora del Refugio (Our Lady of the Refuge, or place of safety). Today many history buffs simply refer to the property as El Refugio (The Refuge).

The grant that established Rancho El Refugio was one of only a few that were given before 1800. Around 1795, Jose Francisco Ortega obtained permission to live on the land (or perhaps to graze it). Ortega was a soldier who had come to Alta California with the Portola expedition in 1769. (The Portola expedition brought Father Junipero Serra, the founder of the Mission Trail, to Alta California. It played an important part in establishing the mission period and gaining control of Alta California for Spain.)

Ortega was a man of many accomplishments. While serving under Portola, he became one of the first non-Indians to set eyes on San Francisco Bay. He is also credited with founding the San Francisco Presidio in 1776. (Presidios were military posts established in California during the Spanish and Mexican periods.) From there he went on to help start Mission Santa Barbara and its presidio ten years later. It was because of deeds like these that he was given the El Refugio grant.

The Ortega rancho bordered the Pacific Ocean, a little more than 20 miles from Santa Barbara Mission. Its shoreline included a small bay, and it is here that many of the property's most interesting stories begin.

One such tale concerns an amazing event that occurred on December 21, 1812, about six years before Bouchard and his men arrived on the scene. As you may know, the year 1812 is famous in California history for the earthquakes that damaged many of southern California's missions. This story is about one of these "shakers."

When the quake struck El Refugio, the trading ship *Mercury* was lying peacefully at anchor in the bay. The *Mercury's* captain was the respected Boston skipper George Washington Ayers. While Ayers was a colorful captain, he was known for keeping an accurate log (the daily record of a ship's voyage). With this in mind, you can bet that some eyebrows were raised when Ayers arrived back in Boston and showed his log to the New England owners of his vessel. The entry for December 21 told a story that may seem hard to believe even today.

According to Ayers' report, the *Mercury* was lying at anchor in approximately six fathoms (36 feet) of water when the quake hit. Suddenly a giant wave lifted the ship and carried it toward the shore. Instead of crashing, the ship was swept up a stream and hurtled inland, into a canyon!

The *Mercury* might have been stranded far from shore, but the retreating wave carried it back to the bay. Ayers noted that his ship was undamaged by its trip up the swollen stream, which an hour earlier a man could have waded across.

As incredible as it sounds, there is good reason to think that this unexpected voyage into a canyon really happened. For one thing, the seagoing ships of 1812 were much smaller and lighter than today's ocean liners. In addition, the quake of December 21, 1812, has been described as "the worst earthquake *and tidal wave* ever recorded" in the Santa Barbara area.

So why was Ayers in little Refugio Bay at the time of the quake in the first place? The answer is that he was trading for skins. At this time Alta California was still controlled by Spain, and it was against the law for citizens

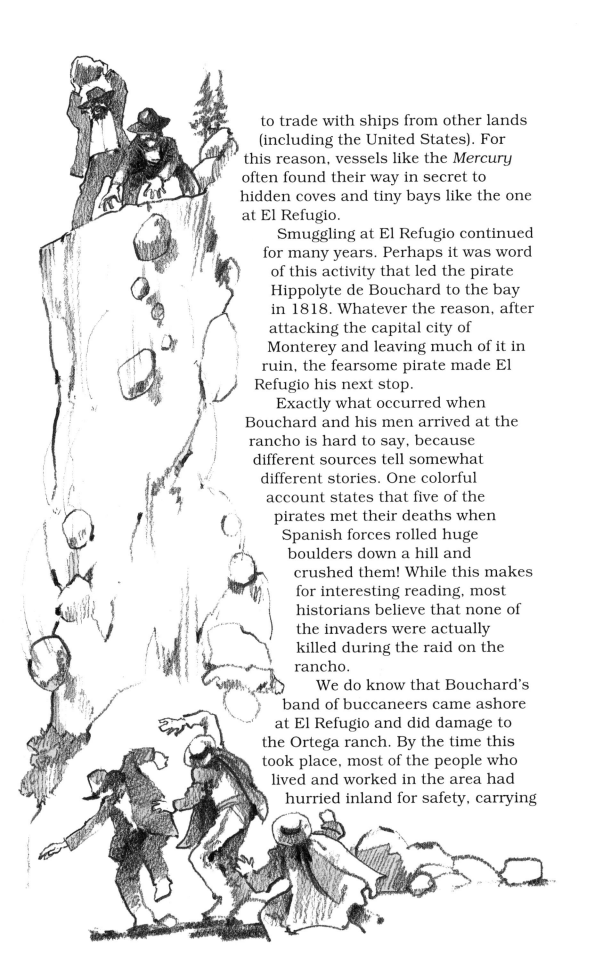

to trade with ships from other lands (including the United States). For this reason, vessels like the *Mercury* often found their way in secret to hidden coves and tiny bays like the one at El Refugio.

Smuggling at El Refugio continued for many years. Perhaps it was word of this activity that led the pirate Hippolyte de Bouchard to the bay in 1818. Whatever the reason, after attacking the capital city of Monterey and leaving much of it in ruin, the fearsome pirate made El Refugio his next stop.

Exactly what occurred when Bouchard and his men arrived at the rancho is hard to say, because different sources tell somewhat different stories. One colorful account states that five of the pirates met their deaths when Spanish forces rolled huge boulders down a hill and crushed them! While this makes for interesting reading, most historians believe that none of the invaders were actually killed during the raid on the rancho.

We do know that Bouchard's band of buccaneers came ashore at El Refugio and did damage to the Ortega ranch. By the time this took place, most of the people who lived and worked in the area had hurried inland for safety, carrying their gold and silver as well as other valuables. (The Ortega family transported their treasures in three Spanish chests. Today the chests are on display in the Santa Ynez historical museum.)

After fleeing the pirates, the local people gathered at the crest of some nearby hills. There they are said to have met soldiers from the Santa Barbara presidio as well as other troops who were returning from their encounter with Bouchard in Monterey. Padres from nearby missions are also reported to have gathered in the outlying hills, along with small groups of Indians they had assembled. But, instead of banding together and pushing the pirates back into the sea, most of the Californians simply watched as the enemy robbed and destroyed the ranch buildings.

Watching from afar may not seem very brave, but the locals may have been outnumbered (or outgunned) by the pirates. After all, Bouchard's two vessels could hold hundreds of men. Even so, not all the Californians were content to sit by while the pirates went about their business. One small group of men (thought to have been vaqueros) did approach the doomed rancho, where they managed to capture three of the pirates. (The unlucky buccaneers are said to have strayed from their mates in search of a cart.)

When Bouchard sailed from El Refugio, the three captives were left behind. It's possible that one of them was a man who went on to make quite a name for himself in California history. More likely, though, the man I'm thinking of simply jumped ship some time during the attack. Either way, Bouchard's loss proved to be California's gain. You might even say that this runaway crew member turned out to be a "treasure" for his new homeland!

This man's name was Joseph Chapman. Originally from the New England area of the United States, Chapman wasn't a pirate by choice. Instead, he had been kidnapped by Bouchard's men while working on the waterfront in Honolulu, Hawaii. He was then forced against his will to serve under the notorious pirate.

From Hawaii Bouchard led his small fleet across the Pacific to California, where he sacked the city of Monterey. According to some accounts, it was there that Chapman either escaped from the pirates or was captured by Californians. Most sources, however, say that El Refugio was the place where Chapman left Bouchard for good.

All sorts of interesting stories have sprung up about how the reluctant pirate became a Californian. According to one colorful tale, Chapman was captured by local vaqueros during the raid on El Refugio. He tried to explain that he had been forced to join Bouchard's crew, but his angry captors didn't speak English. Unable to make out what he was saying, they decided to put him to death! Depending on which version you believe, the unhappy seafarer was going to be hanged, shot, or dragged behind a horse through the countryside.

Just in the nick of time (so the story goes), Jose Ortega's beautiful daughter, Guadalupe, flung herself in front of the condemned man. Declaring that she loved him, she refused to leave his side. If the Californians were going to kill the *gringo* (American), she cried, they would have to kill her first!

Naturally, Ortega was impressed by his daughter's bravery and her affection for the handsome captive. Gesturing to his men, the ranchero ordered them to free the prisoner. In time Joseph and Guadalupe were married. And, as in most good fairy tales, they lived happily ever after.

Unfortunately, most history buffs believe that this exciting tale is more fiction than fact. Another account is probably closer to the truth. According to this story, Chapman wasn't captured by the vaqueros. Instead, he sneaked away from the pirate crew when they came ashore to sack El Refugio. After hiding in the chaparral (thickets of brush) during the day, he made his way under the cover of darkness to Mission Santa Ines, about 11 miles inland. Upon reaching the safety of the mission church, he found it crowded with women and children who had fled from Santa Barbara for fear of attack by the pirates.

While at Santa Ines, Chapman met with the padres and explained how he had escaped from Bouchard. When local authorities heard his story, they told Chapman that he could remain in California, on one condition. He had to be sponsored by a qualified resident.

Chapman found his sponsor in Antonio Maria Lugo, a former officer at the Santa Barbara Presidio. Lugo took the wayward seaman to Los Angeles and put him to work near Mission San Gabriel. There Chapman was kept busy with a variety of projects, including planting vineyards (grapevines) and building grist mills (mills for grinding grain).

Chapman was a skilled craftsman and a hard worker, and his talents soon caught the eye of the padres at San Gabriel. They wasted little time in seeking his help at the mission. Before long he had more work than he could handle.

Thankful to be free of Bouchard and his roughneck crew, Chapman was eager to please the people he met on shore. He became popular with his fellow workers and with other Spanish-speaking Californians, who called him

Jose el Ingles (Joseph the Englishman) because of the language he spoke. (Of course, he was actually an American.)

As Chapman continued to work hard and share his skills, word of the talents and friendliness of "Joseph the Englishman" spread far beyond the San Gabriel area. Presently the padres at Mission Santa Ines requested that he return north to help in building a grist mill.

So it was that Chapman arrived back at the very church where he had first sought refuge from Bouchard. There he was quick to show his appreciation to the padres who had believed his story and helped him stay in California. Happily he set to work building the mill. And, according to this account, it was during this time that he met Guadalupe Ortega, whose family attended church at the mission.

This story certainly seems a bit more realistic than the one I mentioned earlier, in which Guadalupe risked her life to save a condemned man she loved at first sight. No matter which account you believe, however, there *is* a "fairy tale" ending to the saga of the unwilling pirate.

You see, Joseph Chapman and Guadalupe Ortega *did* get married. The happy event took place at Mission Santa Ines in 1822. People from miles around attended the wedding, and the feasting and fun are said to have lasted for several days.

It was about this time, four years after Bouchard's attack on El Refugio, that Mexico was assuming control of California. Having been granted his "freedom" by the government, Chapman was no longer regarded as a pirate. He was welcome to stay in his adopted country, and he could even consider trying to become a citizen someday.

In the meantime Chapman moved to the Los Angeles area, where he lived with his rapidly growing family. There the former Yankee continued to work hard and to help others. After much thought, in 1829 he finally decided to become a citizen.

To help his case, Chapman armed himself with statements from several respected residents, including the padres at Mission San Gabriel. Challenging anyone to find fault with the way he had lived since coming to California, he asked the Mexican government to grant him citizenship.

While he was waiting for the authorities to reply, Chapman busied himself by building an ocean-going schooner (a type of sailing ship with two or more masts). More than one account indicates that he built the vessel at Mission San Gabriel. Now, I know it may seem odd for a schooner to be built at a mission. In the case of San Gabriel, though, it's odder still—the mission is more than two dozen miles from the sea!

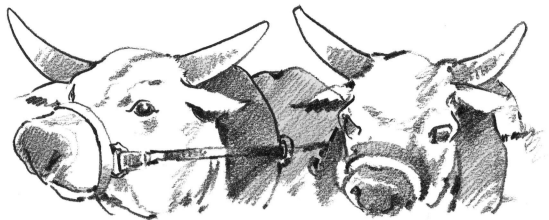

All the same, Chapman completed the task. When he was satisfied that the vessel was seaworthy, the talented craftsman transported it to the Pacific. One account states that he used oxen to haul the completed ship overland. Another says that he took the ship apart to make it easier to transport. Then he hauled the pieces to the port of San Pedro, where he put the vessel back together again.

Either way, the ship arrived safely. Before launching it into the ocean, Joseph proudly named it the *Guadalupe*, after his beloved wife.

With the building of the *Guadalupe*, Joseph Chapman added a historic feat to the story of his life, for his schooner was one of the very first such vessels to be built in California. (Historians disagree about whether it was the first or the second.) The ship was quite large for its day, with accounts listing it at anywhere from 60 to 99 tons. It is reported to have made many successful voyages up and down the Pacific Coast.

The building of the *Guadalupe* was only one of the highlights of Chapman's 30-plus years in California. Certainly, one memorable event for the former New Englander was receiving his citizenship papers in 1831. Soon after that he moved his family back to the Santa Barbara area. For the rest of his life, he continued to add to his list of accomplishments.

It's almost time to bring this chapter to a close, so I'll just tell you briefly about some of the former pirate's many achievements. Showing a talent for building sturdy

adobe structures, Chapman constructed a number of
them. Most of them even stood up to earthquakes. He was
also known for his blacksmithing and carpentry skills,
which he had learned at an early age. In time he gained a
name for his know-how in many other areas, too. As a
doctor, he helped the sick. He even performed surgeries!
As an engineer, he built irrigation systems (waterways)
and reservoirs. As a mason, he built many stone
structures. Some of his constructions, such as the walls of
the Santa Ines grist mill, can still be seen today.

As I've already hinted, Chapman gave much of his
time and labor to the missions while living in the areas
around San Gabriel, Santa Ines, and Santa Barbara. His
work at the missions included helping the padres
construct a number of outlying structures. In Los Angeles,
for example, he is reported to have built a chapel. In
addition, it was Joseph Chapman who cut and shaped the
timbers for the beautiful Los Angeles Plaza Church.
Fittingly, when he died in 1849, he was buried in the
cemetery at Mission Santa Barbara.

Besides being generous with his skills and hard work,
Chapman was dedicated to his family. (You might even
say that he and his beloved Guadalupe *did* live happily
ever after!) Strangely enough—considering that he was
brought to California by a pirate attack on a rancho—he
also became a well-known and respected ranchero. In
1838 Juan Bautista Alvarado, the governor of Mexican
California, granted Chapman 4,438 acres known as

Rancho San Pedro. (Sources disagree about the rancho's location, but it was either in Santa Barbara or Ventura county.)

So you see, Bouchard's lost pirate did turn out to be a "treasure" for his new land. A famous historian probably summed it up best. "Among all the earliest pioneers of California," this historian wrote, "there was no more attractive character, no more useful and popular man, than Joseph Chapman."

With the end of this chapter almost upon us, it's fun to look back and to think about the strange twist it has taken. In the beginning we talked about Rancho El Refugio as the only rancho to be attacked by pirates. As you remember, by the time of the raid on the property, the local people had already taken many of their most valuable belongings to safety. So, Bouchard and his men ended up getting very little for their trouble. With this in mind, and considering all that Joseph Chapman gave to California, it's safe to say that this was one time when a pirate *left more than he took!*

RANCHO SAN JOAQUIN AND MORE

Rancho San Joaquin is located in Orange County. It was made up of two separate parcels (Cienega de las Ranas and La Bolsa de San Joaquin). The properties were granted to Jose Andres Sepulveda in 1837 and 1842. The two parcels amounted to approximately 48,803 acres. The name honors Saint Joachim.

Fast Horses and Buried Treasures

I thought it might be fun to begin this chapter by following the fiery French pirate Hippolyte de Bouchard down the California coast. After leaving El Refugio, he made a brief stop at nearby Santa Barbara. There he arranged for an exchange of prisoners. (The crafty buccaneer was able to get three of his men back for one prisoner of his own.) As part of the "deal," Bouchard promised to leave California without making any more attacks.

This, however, was not to be. After the prisoner exchange was completed, Bouchard turned up next near Mission San Juan Capistrano and continued to pillage and plunder. As with the other places where his men came ashore, local people are said to have buried assorted treasures to hide them from the pirates before fleeing for safety.

Most of those who left San Juan Capistrano headed for Rancho Trabuco. Old stories say that the rancho was a place where mission valuables were taken for safekeeping during the Bouchard raid. If you like hunting for treasure, you might be interested in knowing that a sizable amount of this mission wealth is said to be hidden in the area to this day!

One tale even hints that a metal box contained a map leading to the fortune. The box was buried beneath the roots of a sycamore tree. Unfortunately, there are hundreds of sycamore trees on the property. So far no one has dug under the right one.

Another treasure tale connected with the Trabuco rancho tells of a treasure that *was* found. According to this account, some time in the 1800s an Indian boy was returning from a cattle drive when he saw a ghostly light flickering in an old adobe house near the center of Rancho Trabuco. The boy became very excited, for he had been told that "tongues of flame" rose and fell over buried treasure!

Hurriedly the boy ran off to tell the man who had sent him on the drive. Together they returned to the site and dug a deep hole. Around daybreak they uncovered a pot filled with Spanish gold coins. Sadly for the boy, his partner soon left the area, taking the fortune with him! Neither the man nor the gold was ever seen again.

Now, this tale does sound more like a colorful legend than a factual story. However, it *is* known that an adobe building once stood where the pot of gold was supposedly found.

In getting back to Bouchard's raid on San Juan, I must admit that there is little of excitement to report. About the only "valuables" the pirates managed to plunder were wine and spirits (liquor), much of which they drank up on the spot. Their activities may have been cut short when soldiers from as far away as Santa Barbara, Los Angeles, and San Diego arrived on the scene. Facing this show of force, Bouchard apparently decided to take his leave. After sailing away from the small bay (known today as Dana's Cove), he was not seen again along the California coast.

Having followed Bouchard to the area around San Juan Capistrano, we find ourselves in Orange County. As you may know, this southern California county is the home of such modern-day "treasures" as Disneyland and Knott's Berry Farm amusement park. You probably know all about Disneyland, but I wonder how many people know that Knott's Berry Farm was built on the Rancho Los Coyotes grant? Orange County contains several other interesting ranchos as well. The next account is about one of these properties, and the fascinating individual who acquired it.

Don Jose Andres Sepulveda is the person I'm thinking of, and his rancho was known as San Joaquin. It was made up of two separate grants and included nearly 49,000 acres. The rancho has an interesting connection with the one discussed in the last chapter. As you may remember, Jose Francisco Ortega's rancho was known as El Refugio (the refuge). Sepulveda gave this same name to the king-sized adobe *casa* (house) he built at San Joaquin.

Besides being a "refuge" for his own family, Sepulveda's house—like many others during rancho days—was a popular gathering place for people from miles around. The property became known far and wide for its fancy entertainment, as well as for the extra-fancy style of clothes that Sepulveda chose to wear.

There were a number of things about Sepulveda that helped to make him one of California's most colorful characters in the years leading up to the Gold Rush. Besides his huge land holdings, his friendliness toward visitors, and his elegant costumes, he was known for his fast race horses and reckless wagers (bets). So it's not surprising that he became involved in one of the most fantastic horse races that California (or any other state) has ever known.

The year of this event was 1852. The Gold Rush was in full swing, and with the arrival of American fortune hunters, Sepulveda's bets were bigger and more reckless than ever. One of his major rivals was Pio Pico, one of California's largest land owners and a man who had twice been governor under Mexican rule.

Now, the former governor had a race horse named Sarco that he was very proud of, and with good reason. The mighty gray stallion proved unbeatable whenever it was entered in a rodeo or other horse racing event. Many of Sarco's victories came against horses owned by Andres Sepulveda, who tried again and again to find a horse that could beat him.

The proud Pico was willing to bet that his stallion could outrun any horse in the state over a nine-mile course. (Nowadays horse races are much shorter, usually less than two miles.) With no horse even coming close to defeating the champion, people from throughout California began boasting that Sarco was the fastest horse in the world.

A sailor who had recently arrived in the Golden State wasn't so sure. While in far-off Australia, he had seen a horse that he thought could beat Sarco. The horse was a mare by the name of Black Swan. According to the sailor, she could run like the wind!

As often happens in stories of this kind, the facts tend to get blurred over the years. For this reason we can't be sure exactly how Andres Sepulveda ended up with the animal. According to one account, Black Swan was bred in Australia but was already in California when Sepulveda acquired her. But there is a second tale that I like better. As the story goes, Sepulveda somehow heard about Black Swan and proceeded to track down the sailor who was talking about her. After hearing firsthand about the fleet-footed mare, he sent a secret agent to Australia to buy her.

Sepulveda met the agent, and the prized race horse, on the San Francisco waterfront. Quietly he took the mare to his rancho. Once he saw her speed and strength, he was sure he had a horse to challenge Sarco at last. Wasting little time, he contacted Pico to arrange a race.

Word of the race, and of the tremendous speed of the Australian-bred challenger, soon spread throughout the region. Proud Californians scoffed at the praise heaped on Black Swan, and they backed up their belief in the unbeatable Sarco with huge wagers. On the other side, numerous newcomers, and people who were familiar with horse racing in other lands, matched the Californians with large bets of their own. But none of these wagers came close to the bet that was made between Andres Sepulveda and Pio Pico.

To begin with, the proud and wealthy rancheros put up $25,000 in gold (an amount equal to several hundred thousand dollars today!). But that wasn't all. To sweeten the pot, they also bet 500 horses, 500 mares, 500 cows, 500 calves, and 500 sheep on the outcome of the race!

As I mentioned earlier, the race was to be nine miles long. It was to start at the Los Angeles Plaza and head in a southerly direction down San Pedro Road. After four and a half miles, the horses were to turn around and race back to the Plaza.

People from throughout California came to Los Angeles to witness the grand event, and to add their bets to the countless wagers being made. Among those who got caught up in the excitement was the wife of Andres Sepulveda. According to one story, she even passed out 50-dollar gold pieces to workers on the San Joaquin Rancho so they could join in the fun!

By the time the great day arrived, people were caught up in a frenzy of arguing and betting. Those who didn't have money (or hidden stashes of gold) made bets with whatever they could lay their hands on. They wagered such prized items as silver-studded saddles and bridles, as well as less valuable things like well-worn blankets and boots. So widespread was the betting that the race was said to affect the fortunes of every family in the area.

When at last the race began, it did seem as if every family was well represented along its course. One gentleman who was there commented, "Everybody in the country was present and the whole country as far north as San Luis Obispo and south to San Diego was depopulated. They had all come to see the great race."

As it turned out, the race truly was great. At first Sarco surged ahead. At the halfway mark, Pico's stallion was still well in the lead, but Black Swan would not give in. As they thundered around the turn and galloped back toward the Los Angeles Plaza, the mighty mare began to close the gap. By the time they reached the three-quarter mark, Sarco's lead had shrunk to about six lengths. (A length is the approximate measure of a horse from head to tail.)

With about a mile and a half to go, Black Swan finally caught up with Sarco. For a lengthy spurt the sweating horses raced head to head as the crowds screamed with excitement, urging on their favorites.

Then, after about eight and a half miles of exhausting racing, Sepulveda's Australian mare began to pull away. Perhaps Black Swan got a second wind, or Sarco just plain tired out. Whatever the reason, by the time she reached the Plaza, Black Swan was in front by 75 yards! The mare's supporters cheered wildly as she crossed the finish line. Of course, no one was happier than Andres Sepulveda. At long last he had found the horse that could beat Pico's champion stallion!

After the cheering was over and the excitement died away, Sepulveda proudly took his gallant mount back to his rancho. There she is said to have stepped on a nail and contracted tetanus (a disease also known as lockjaw). All too soon the great mare was dead.

Even though Black Swan's life was cut short, her victory over Sarco remains one of southern California's most memorable sporting events. Sadly, it was also one of Andres Sepulveda's last moments of glory. In the years that followed, he suffered problems with money because of his free-spending way of life, his generous hospitality, and his large gambling losses. As his debts piled up and he was unable to pay them, he was forced to sell Rancho San Joaquin.

The land was sold in 1864 to James Irvine, Llewellyn Bixby, and Benjamin and Thomas Flint. Twelve years later, Irvine bought out his partners. Combined with several other nearby properties, the rancho's land became known as Irvine Ranch. This vast holding stretched to more than 100,000 acres and covered approximately one-fourth of Orange County!

James Irvine died in 1886. In time the management of the giant estate was passed to his son, James Irvine, Jr. The younger James formed the Irvine Company in 1894. It is this company that continues to control many thousands of acres of the original ranch property. Thanks to the company, and the two Irvines, this vast acreage became known as one of the last great ranches in California.

Today there are giant developments sprinkled about the original ranch holdings. Among these are business and research institutions, large communities of homes, and parks and recreational facilities. The Irvine campus of the University of California is also located there, as are a number of towns (including the community of Irvine).

Even with all the building that has taken place on thousands of acres of the Irvine Ranch, parts of the original property are still ranch-like. If you visit the area, you can see cattle grazing in open fields, as well as crops of various kinds and many acres of orchards. Unfortunately, this may soon change as more and more people and buildings gobble up the historic ranch land.

With this change of scene bringing sadness to history buffs, let me end this chapter on a happier note, at least for treasure seekers. According to a story known to fortune hunters, somewhere on Irvine Ranch a lost stagecoach treasure is buried!

Tradition states that this loot (said to be worth about $30,000 today) was robbed from the northbound San Diego stage in 1868. Five masked highwaymen ambushed the coach as it made its way through a tree-lined canyon near the community of Corona del Mar. After demanding the strongbox containing the valuables, the bandits waved the stage on.

The stagecoach driver's next stop was the town of Santa Ana. There he immediately reported the robbery to the sheriff. With a posse at his heels, the sheriff lit out for the nearby Santa Ana Mountains, where he thought the outlaws would hide. Although they searched through the night, the sheriff and his men couldn't find any sign of a trail.

Tired and discouraged, the sheriff decided to call off the hunt and return to Santa Ana. As the posse traveled along a small spring near the site of the robbery, suddenly they stumbled across the bandits, still wrapped in their blankets! Not bothering to announce their arrival, the lawmen pulled their pistols from their holsters and started firing. With barely enough time to stagger out of their bedrolls, the five outlaws were killed on the spot.

Unfortunately, a search of the bandits' camp failed to turn up any sign of the strongbox. To this day the location of the treasure remains a mystery.

Interestingly, there *is* one clue to the whereabouts of the lost stagecoach loot. According to an old-timer's tale, after the killings the spring became known as "Sheriff's Spring." A second source indicates that this spring is located somewhere on the grounds of the Irvine branch of the University of California.

So, if you ever visit this beautiful campus, you might want to have a look around. Good luck, and don't forget to get permission before you dig!

6 NEW HELVETIA

New Helvetia is located in Sacramento, Yuba, and Sutter Counties. It was first granted to John Augustus Sutter in 1841. The original grant was for approximately 48,839 acres. The name means New Switzerland.

If It Wasn't for Beppo . . .

In the last chapter, the tale of Andres Sepulveda and Rancho San Joaquin brought us up to Gold Rush times. As you may already know, the discovery of gold was one of the most important happenings in the history of California. But did you know that the story of this event begins with the grant of a California rancho?

The rancho I'm thinking of had the unusual name of New Helvetia. It was granted to one of the most famous people in California history, a man named John Augustus Sutter. If it wasn't for Sutter, gold wouldn't have been discovered when and where it was. And if it wasn't for a bulldog named Beppo . . .

But I'm getting ahead of myself here. Let me back up and tell you how Sutter came to California in the first place, and what happened to him after he established his rancho. I think you'll agree that it's quite a story.

The tale begins in 1839, when a youthful man (in his mid 30s) arrived in Mexican California wearing a dazzling

uniform that had once belonged to a French army officer. The dashing young man presented himself as a former captain in the Swiss army (in the European country of Switzerland). Not only that, but he claimed to be a war hero, besides.

The truth is that the likable and talkative gentleman was neither an officer nor a war hero. Instead, he was wanted by the Swiss police! It seems that he owed quite a bit of money to other people and wasn't able to pay his debts. Five years earlier, he had fled to America to avoid being arrested and sent to debtor's prison. Strangely enough, he went on to become one of the greatest landowners in the history of California—and perhaps the entire United States!

This man was, of course, John Augustus Sutter. Born in Germany in 1803, Sutter grew up in the neighboring country of Switzerland. It was this country that he considered his homeland.

By the time he reached California, Sutter had already worked at a number of trades in various parts of the United States. Although some of the things he tried made money, others didn't. By 1838 he was broke again and in need of another fresh start.

It was then that Sutter decided to go to the Pacific Coast. During a long and dangerous journey across the continent, he heard about a lush valley in Alta California. (We call it the Sacramento Valley today.) Some say that it was the description of this beautiful land, and its plentiful wildlife, that started him thinking about establishing a settlement there.

Sutter's cross-country travels took him to a place called Fort Vancouver, a fur trading post in the Oregon Territory. When he was told that it was too late in the year to travel overland to the Sacramento Valley, he looked for a ship that was sailing for California. Not finding one, he decided to board a vessel that was headed for the Sandwich Islands (present-day Hawaii) instead. From there he hoped to catch a second ship that would take him to California.

Sutter ended up staying in Hawaii for five months. As things turned out, his lengthy stopover worked out for the best. For one thing, he was able to acquire goods that he would need for his settlement. More important, he had plenty of time to think about his Sacramento Valley dream—and to talk about it, too.

Soon the eager young Swiss aroused the interest of a handful of Americans and native Kanakas (Hawaiians) in his project. It was this group that sailed with him to California, although they ended up taking a roundabout route—by way of Alaska! Also making the long journey was an English bulldog that Sutter had become attached to. He called the dog Beppo.

After arriving in San Francisco Bay, Sutter's ship was sent farther south, to the capital community of Monterey (the official port of entry to Alta California). There he met with Governor Juan B. Alvarado. Welcoming Sutter's plans for a Sacramento Valley settlement, Alvarado urged him to take out citizenship papers, locate the land he wanted, and begin his project.

With the governor's blessings, it was a happy John Augustus Sutter who left Monterey to begin searching for a site for his new home. He planned to return at a later date to receive his Mexican citizenship, along with an official grant of land.

To start his search, Sutter chartered (rented) three small boats. Loading them with people and supplies, he began exploring. For a number of days he traveled up the Sacramento River, eagerly observing the wildlife, the beautiful scenery, and the curious Indians who watched from the river banks. Then he left the Sacramento River and ventured up the Rio Americano (American River). About two miles from where the two rivers meet, he ordered his little fleet to stop. After looking over the area, he decided that he had found the place to build his settlement.

With Sutter leading the way, the settlers and boatmen set to work unloading equipment and setting up camp. Early the next morning, the crews of the chartered boats made ready to leave. The valley might be pretty, but they couldn't wait to escape the August heat, not to mention the mosquitoes!

To bid farewell to the boatmen, Sutter fired a thunderous nine-gun salute from the three brass cannons he had brought to the site. The boat crews responded with a hearty "Hip-hip-hooray!" According to William Davis, one of the boat captains, all this noise created quite a scene. Startled by the sounds, deer, elk, and other wild animals began running about in panic, while wolves and coyotes howled in the nearby woods. Overhead, huge flocks of birds flew wildly about the camp.

It wasn't only the animals who were startled. Indians in the area were also awed by the sounds. Later on, several of them told Sutter that his salute to the boat crews may have saved his life. It seems that the Indians had been planning to attack his camp. After hearing the booming cannons, they changed their minds!

With the boats having departed, Sutter and his workers began the task of turning the area near their campsite into a permanent settlement. In addition to the Kanakas and other workers who were already with him, Sutter made friends with some of the local Indians and coaxed them into helping with the work. Together the men set about making adobe bricks and clearing a path to the Sacramento River.

As the workers labored in the summer heat, a large building began to take shape. In time this building was enclosed by massive walls complete with two bastions (tower-like structures) and a number of gun ports (openings to shoot through in case of attack). With its bastions and high, thick walls, the structure looked more like a fortress than someone's home. Later on it would be given the nickname "Sutter's Fort."

Inside the walls of the fort, other structures were added to house such things as a bakery, a blanket factory, a mill, and a distillery (used to make liquor from

wheat and grapes). There were shops for coopers (barrel makers), carpenters, shoe makers, blacksmiths, and saddle makers. Also located within the walls were storerooms and barracks (living areas for workers).

While all this building was going on inside the fort, Sutter was also busy developing the land outside. He and his men cleared fields and planted wheat, orchards, and vineyards. In addition, they began raising livestock, including cattle and horses.

Along the way Sutter found time to return to Monterey. There he was granted his Mexican citizenship, along with the ownership of more than 48,000 acres of land for his wilderness outpost. In honor of his homeland, he proudly called his rancho Nueva Helvetia, a name made up of the Spanish word for "new" and the ancient Roman word for Switzerland.

During the next few years, Sutter more than tripled his land holdings, acquiring a Russian outpost called Fort Ross as well as a huge area of land that was given to him by Governor Manuel Micheltorena. The once-penniless Swiss had become the ruler of a truly kingly domain!

Sutter was not a typical California ranchero. Other large landowners spent much of their time raising cattle, trading in hide and tallow, and having fiestas. Like them, Sutter did raise large numbers of livestock, and he dealt in hides. In fact, one source indicates that he owned approximately 12,000 cattle, 2,500 horses, 2,000 sheep, 1,000 hogs, and 70 mules. But instead of trading all the skins to Boston ship captains, he built a tannery and made leather from the hides. And even though there were festive social gatherings at New Helvetia, Sutter seemed most interested in building his fort, adding to his lands, and doing business with newcomers to his inland kingdom.

In the years leading up to the Gold Rush, Sutter's Fort became a gathering place where trail-weary travelers could buy supplies, replace livestock, and renew their spirits. Sutter did his best to make sure visitors felt welcome and enjoyed their stay. Generous and free-spending, he also had a habit of hiring many of the people who came to his fort—especially if they were skilled in a particular trade or craft.

As more and more foreigners were attracted to his growing empire, Sutter began having trouble with Mexican officials. He welcomed and encouraged settlers from other countries, and he was friendly with Americans. This was at a time when Mexican officials in California were becoming nervous about the many newcomers arriving in their land, especially those from the United States.

There was good reason for the government to be nervous. By the early 1840s, the neighboring countries of Mexico and the United States had been feuding for many years. Americans were pouring into the frontier, and their country was expanding. Mexico correctly feared that the United States might try to take some of its territory.

In 1846 the two nations went to war. Even before word of the conflict reached California, a group of Americans staged the famed Bear Flag Revolt against the Mexican government. Beginning with the revolt, Sutter's rancho became the scene of several warlike happenings. For a brief time, a party of Americans took over his fort and used it as a place to keep prisoners, including the well-known Mexican citizen Mariano Guadalupe Vallejo. (One of these Americans was the famous explorer and soldier John Charles Frémont. We'll meet Frémont again in the next chapter.) Sutter disapproved of these actions, but there was little he could do about them. To his credit, he treated his "prisoners" as honored guests.

When the Bear Flaggers learned that the United States was at war with Mexico, they abandoned their "California Republic" to join the American cause. The Stars and Stripes were raised over the fort at New Helvetia, and many of Sutter's best men joined Frémont's California Battalion of Volunteers. As part of the battalion, they fought in battles that took place far from the Sacramento Valley.

During much of this troubled time Sutter remained at New Helvetia. When the war ended, the United States was in control of Alta California. The days of Mexican rule were over.

As Sutter's men returned to the fort, he warmly welcomed them home. They went back to work on the settlement, proud of the American victory and the part they had played in it. With the coming of peace, New Helvetia enjoyed a time of growth and good will.

Meanwhile, people continued to find their way to Sutter's Fort. By the middle of 1847, Sutter realized that he needed more lumber for his building projects. Thinking that a water-powered sawmill would help solve his problem, he decided to build one on a nearby river. To do this he needed to team up with someone who had the right skills to help build the mill.

The man Sutter chose as his partner was James Wilson Marshall. Originally from the state of New Jersey, Marshall had arrived at Sutter's Fort (by way of the Oregon Territory) in 1845. A man of many talents, he was especially skilled as a carpenter. Sutter thought he was just the right man to supervise the construction of the sawmill.

Marshall soon set out from New Helvetia to find a good location for the mill. After some searching, he found the place he was looking for on the South Fork of the American River, about 45 miles from Sutter's Fort. With Sutter's approval, the building of the mill began.

Little did either man know that they were setting the stage for one of the most important discoveries in our nation's history. It happened on January 24, 1848, when James Wilson Marshall found gold at the mill site!

You might think that the gold find would be a bonanza for Sutter. Instead, the discovery marked the beginning of the end of his dream of an inland empire.

With the cry of "Gold!" echoing throughout the world, people from far and near rushed to California by land and

by sea. Many of them headed for Sutter's settlement on the American River. Unfortunately, Sutter could not control the huge number of people who came to his fort. Greedy gold seekers made themselves at home on his land. They trampled his gardens, ate his food, killed his cattle, and stole his belongings.

As more and more gold-hungry people arrived, things went from bad to worse. Sutter's losses mounted until he was unable to pay his bills or to keep many of the promises he had made. Finally, he was forced to sell his beloved fort, along with much of the surrounding land. (It was on part of this property that the town of Sacramento sprang up. In 1854 Sacramento became California's state capital.)

Sadly, Sutter moved his homestead from his fort to another part of his vast holdings, a site on the Feather River called Hock Farm. There he lived with his Swiss wife and several other family members who had joined him in California. Putting bad times behind him, he was able to enjoy a period of happiness.

During this time Sutter traveled to Monterey and served as a delegate to California's constitutional convention (a meeting called to draft the state constitution). In October, 1849, the new constitution was signed. This event gave Sutter one of his greatest moments. Filled with pride and joy, he sprang from his seat in the convention hall. "Gentlemen," he exclaimed, "this is the happiest day of my life!" As tears streamed down his face, he added, "This is a great day for California!"

Unfortunately, that memorable day may have been one of Sutter's last truly happy times. He tried running for governor of the new state, only to lose a close election to his former lawyer. Worse, a fire broke out at Hock Farm and destroyed the main house along with many of Sutter's belongings.

After the fire, Sutter and his wife decided to leave California. Moving all the way to the opposite side of the United States, they settled in the little town of Lititz, Pennsylvania. It was there that one of California's most famous pioneers spent his last years.

Angry over the way things had turned out in California, Sutter decided to seek help from the government. Traveling to Washington, D.C., he asked the United States Congress for money to make up for his losses during the Mexican-American War and the property he had lost to gold-seeking squatters.

Sad to say, Sutter never received the money he felt was owed to him. In June, 1880, the one-time leader of New Helvetia rancho died, a broken and bitter man.

Sutter's last days may have been unhappy, but he had made a huge mark in the history of California—and of much of the world, too. If it wasn't for Sutter and the growth of his Sacramento Valley settlement, James Marshall would not have set out to build a sawmill on the South Fork of the American River. And without Marshall's discovery of gold, there's no telling when or where the

Gold Rush might have taken place. Gold seekers from around the world would not have left their homes when they did. Perhaps the town of Sacramento, which was built on land that Sutter once owned, would never have come to be. All we can say for sure is that the story of the Golden State would have been very different.

These thoughts bring me back to the title of this chapter. If you remember Beppo, Sutter's English bulldog, you've probably been wondering what he has to do with this story. Well, after traveling with Sutter from Hawaii to Alaska, and then to California, Beppo proved to be more than a favored pet. In the early days of Sutter's Fort, the little-known bulldog is reported to have saved his master's life—and not once, but twice! Both occasions were the result of attacks by Indians.

Now, let's pause a moment to think about this. Saving anyone's life would have been enough to make Beppo special. But because the life he saved was that of John Augustus Sutter, the faithful bulldog did something that changed the course of history.

As we've already talked about, *if it wasn't for Sutter*, and his need for more lumber, gold would not have been discovered when and where it was. And if Sutter had died in the early days of the settlement, New Helvetia would have come to an end. There would have been no need for a sawmill, and James Marshall would have been doing something else on that famous day in January, 1848, instead of finding gold.

So when we remember John Augustus Sutter and his place in history, we should also remember his loyal bulldog. After all, *if it wasn't for Beppo* . . .

7 RANCHO LAS MARIPOSAS

Rancho Las Mariposas is located in Mariposa County. It was first granted in 1844 to Juan Bautista Alvarado. The original grant was for approximately 44,387 acres. *Mariposa* is the Spanish word for butterfly.

A Golden Mistake

One of the things about history that fascinates me is how often one tale leads to another. One example is the story of the famed explorer and soldier John Charles Frémont. You may remember that we met this pioneer pathfinder briefly in the last chapter, on John Augustus Sutter and New Helvetia. Frémont was with the forces that occupied Sutter's Fort for a time during the American takeover of California. But that's not the only thing connecting these two famous men.

When most people think of Sutter, they also think of gold (even though Sutter himself lost more than he gained from the gold discovery). Well, the precious yellow metal is another connection between the ill-fated Swiss ranchero and the American explorer.

You see, like Sutter, Frémont also acquired a rancho, one that came complete with its own hidden store of yellow riches. The strange part is, it wasn't the rancho that Frémont set out to buy. In fact, you might say that he lucked into his treasure because of *a golden mistake!*

The treasure-filled property is called Las Mariposas. It is also referred to as the Mariposa Grant. *Mariposa* is the Spanish word for butterfly, and the name can be traced back to an expedition led by Gabriel Moraga in the early 1800s.

Moraga was a well-known explorer of northern California and the great Central Valley during Spanish times. As the story goes, Moraga and his men made camp one day by a stream in the Sierra foothills. There they were visited by thousands of butterflies. The Spaniards were very impressed with the number and beauty of these tiny creatures—so much so that they named the stream after them. Today that stream, a town the stream flows through, and a Gold Country county are all known by the name Mariposa.

The original Mariposa grant was given to Juan Bautista Alvarado, a former governor of Mexican California, in 1844. (And that's another interesting connection. As you may remember from the last chapter, it was Governor Alvarado who encouraged John Augustus Sutter to settle in the Sacramento Valley.) In 1847 the property was acquired by a man who was acting as an agent for the real buyer, John Charles Frémont.

Known throughout the United States for his explorations in the Far West, Frémont had a number of nicknames given to him over the years. Perhaps the best known is "the Pathfinder." He gained this name in part from the number of expeditions he led to California. One of his accomplishments was managing to cross the rugged Sierra Nevada in the dead of winter (a feat some said couldn't be done).

Frémont certainly did endure some rough times in the wilderness. Still, the name of Pathfinder may be misleading.

According to some of the men who accompanied him on his journeys, he actually found few new paths himself. In fact, he sometimes needed help staying on paths that had been blazed by others. The "Pathfinder" was lucky to have the help of some of the West's most respected mountain men, who acted as guides for his expeditions. (Two of these legendary explorers were Kit Carson and Joseph Walker. You might like to read about these men in other books.)

But whether or not he was a great trailblazer, Frémont certainly was a man of action. It seems as if we run across his name wherever colorful (and sometimes questionable) events were happening during the time when the United States was taking over control of California.

One of these events happened at a place called Hawk's Peak. Now known as Frémont Peak, the mountain overlooks the mission town of San Juan Bautista. At the time of the Hawk's Peak incident (March, 1846), tension was growing between Americans in California and the Mexican government. So it was insulting to government officials

(not to mention risky) when Frémont built a log fort on the peak and raised an American flag over it—especially since he was an officer in the United States Army at the time! It was almost as if the brash soldier was thumbing his nose at the authorities. To make matters worse, Hawk's Peak was only about 25 miles from Monterey, the capital of Mexican California.

It was a short time later that Frémont became involved in the famed Bear Flag Revolt. (You may remember that we talked about this episode briefly in the New Helvetia chapter.) The uprising took place before the people involved knew that the United States and Mexico were at war. The rebels were a small group of men, mostly Americans, who tried to seize control of California. Their idea was to create an independent country they called the Bear Flag Republic. (The rebels' famous banner later provided the basic design for the California state flag, which was officially adopted in 1911.)

Shortly after the revolt broke out, news reached the Bear Flaggers that the United States was officially at war with Mexico. Once again the busy Mr. Frémont leapt into action. His California Battalion of Volunteers became associated with the regular United States forces. Named a major by U.S. Commodore Robert Field Stockton, Frémont led his battalion into the fray.

Frémont wasn't involved in the war's most bitterly fought battles. But when the war ended, the Pathfinder was in the right place at the right time. It was John

Charles Frémont who accepted the Mexican surrender at Cahuenga that ended the fighting in California.

After the war, Stockton named Frémont military governor of California. Unfortunately, his term was a short one. Frémont thought he was supposed to be in charge in California, but U.S. General Stephen Watts Kearny had his own orders to organize a government. When Frémont refused to obey Kearny, the Pathfinder was charged with mutiny!

Frémont was stripped of his title of military governor and forced to stand trial in far-off Washington, D.C. There he was found guilty by a military court.

Fortunately for Frémont, at this point President James K. Polk stepped into the picture and granted him a pardon. By this time, though, the frustrated officer was so angry that he resigned from the army.

Frémont had more than one reason for being fed up. In addition to his trial and conviction in Washington, he was also upset about some property he had bought back in California.

This land was, of course, Las Mariposas. It was composed of more than 44,000 acres of hot, dry land in the foothills of the Sierra Nevada mountain range. What Frémont actually wanted to buy was some property much closer to the coast. So how did he end up with a rancho so different from the kind of land he had his eyes on? Well, the story is a little confusing, and hard to piece together even today.

Old documents show that Frémont didn't buy his rancho directly. Instead, he asked another man to act as his agent. Now, the agent was supposed to find some property near Mission San Jose, or perhaps somewhere around either San Francisco or Monterey Bay. (You can take your pick, because different sources give different locations.) For reasons that are still unclear, Frémont's agent used his money to buy property in the Sierra foothills instead.

So it was an angry John Charles Frémont who set off for California, ready to go to court in order to straighten things out. But while he was on his way West, some startling news reached him. On or near his unwanted land, gold had been found! Not only that, but a major gold strike had been made in the Sierras north of his property.

As you can imagine, Frémont suddenly had second thoughts about selling his land. First he would check to see just how much gold might be found on the rancho.

The answer turned out to be . . . quite a bit! In fact, the property that he had bought for $3,000 contained gold worth *millions* of dollars!

With this happy turn of events, Frémont eagerly took on the task of overseeing his land. Soon he was stretching the boundaries of his property as far as he could. While doing this, he claimed land that was being worked by other prospectors. So he ended up in court after all, this time to defend his ownership of property that was also claimed by others.

In the end, the Pathfinder won his court battles, but he made many enemies along the way. Life in the Gold Country was proving to be anything but peaceful. Still, it *was* making him very rich.

With the help of his wife, Jessie, Frémont worked his holdings to get all the treasure out of them that he could. He hired a number of men to help him with such things as keeping his grant free of uninvited guests, panning the streams, and gathering the surface gold. He also introduced newer ways of mining to help in removing the precious metal from the ground.

Unfortunately, the richer Las Mariposas proved to be, the more Frémont was resented by other miners who thought he had "stolen" their claims. One organization that backed this group of angry prospectors was the Merced Mining Company. This company had operated several money-making mines within the boundaries of Frémont's Mariposa grant.

Then things reached a boiling point. An enraged gang of gold seekers (and hangers on) went on the attack. They seized part of the Frémont property and blocked the roads leading to the family home, which was located in an area known as Bear Valley.

Frémont knew that he and his men were greatly outnumbered. Their only hope was to get outside help. But with the roads blocked, it seemed no one would be able to get through. Things looked bleak for the trapped family and the crew of workers.

At this point a couple of unlikely heroes come into the tale. John and Jessie Frémont had a 15-year-old daughter named Lily. Also with the family was a teenage boy from England. His name was Douglass Fox, and he was visiting the rancho when the trouble began. Together this young pair secretly worked out a plan to get help.

As night began to fall, the two teenagers slipped out of the house and made their way to the stable. There they saddled Lily's favorite horse. After darkness had set in, Douglass led the animal to a dry creek-bed behind the

house. When no one sounded an alarm, he knew he was safe—so far.

Slowly and ever so quietly, the English lad then led the horse up a brush-covered hill. As he came over the hilltop, out of sight of the house, he mounted the animal and began a long and dangerous dash for help. His destination was Coulterville, a mining town about 20 miles to the north.

All through the night, Frémont did his best to encourage his men and keep them alert. Then a frightening message arrived from the miners who were besieging the property.

It came in the form of a note to Jessie. The message said that she and her children must leave the property within 24 hours—or be burned out! The note demanded that she reply by sundown.

Naturally, Jessie was frightened for her family's safety, and she was worried about Douglass Fox as well. But she was a courageous woman, and she refused to respond to the note. Instead, she clung to the hope that young Douglass would reach Coulterville and that help would come in time.

As the hours ticked by, the blazing sun drove the heat to a scorching 115 degrees. Throughout the long, hot day Jessie kept watch, hoping and praying for rescuers to arrive.

Finally, as the sun was about to set, a tired and saddle-sore Douglass Fox crept into the Frémont house. With a weary grin of triumph, he told the family they should hold out. He had made it to Coulterville, and help was on the way! Even better, a messenger was continuing on to the community of Stockton, where a telegraph would be sent to the governor to tell him what was happening in Bear Valley.

When Jessie heard the news, she almost cried with joy. Then, without giving a thought to her own safety, she set out to reply to the Frémonts' enemies—in person!

Putting on her finest clothes, Jessie told her driver to fetch the family's best carriage and prepare the horses for an outing. When all was ready, Jessie, along with the driver and her French maid, headed for the village saloon, where the leaders of the uprising had gathered.

At the saloon, Jessie signalled for her driver to stop and demanded to see the saloon's owner (a man who had sided with the miners). When he came out, followed by several other men, Jessie handed him the miners' note. There would be *no* answer to their demand, she announced, because what they were doing was against the law. Her voice rising, she added, "You may come and kill us, we are but women and children and it will be easy—but you cannot kill the Law!" She finished her brief speech by telling the astounded miners and onlookers that help was on the way and their game was up.

Jessie's bold display of courage threw the miners into confusion. Some of them argued for attacking immediately and driving the Frémonts out before reinforcements arrived. Others wanted to wait and see what the governor had to say. As the groups squabbled, the spirit of the siege was broken. The Battle of Bear Valley, as the incident came to be known, was over.

Of course, there is much more to the story of Las Mariposas and its colorful owners than I can squeeze into this chapter. Perhaps you'll want to read more on your own about John Charles and Jessie Frémont, or about the many mines that were worked in and about their property.

In bringing this chapter to a close, I do want to mention that the man known as the Pathfinder continued to make history in later years. Among other noteworthy accomplishments, he returned to Washington to serve as one of California's first United States senators. In 1856, he became the first person nominated for U.S. president by the brand-new Republican Party. (He lost the election to James Buchanan. In 1860, the Republicans won the presidency for the first time with their next candidate, Abraham Lincoln.)

In the early 1860s Frémont attracted still more attention (and was involved in still more controversy) as an officer in the Civil War. Some years later, he also served as governor of the Territory of Arizona.

Certainly both fame and fortune came to John Charles Frémont during his eventful life. Sadly, however, his last years remind me again of John Augustus Sutter, who lost his fortune and died far from California. Through bad luck and bad investments, Frémont's fabulous wealth all but disappeared. When he died during a trip East in 1890, the 77-year-old Pathfinder was alone and nearly broke in a New York City boarding house.

As for the courageous Jessie, she lived another dozen years in Los Angeles before passing away in 1902, at the age of 78. In the later years of the Frémonts' life together, it was Jessie's talents that provided money for the family, as she became a widely read writer.

Today the name Frémont lives on, and not just in history books or in the local lore of Las Mariposas. You can be sure that the proud Pathfinder won't be forgotten any time soon, for it's said that more streets, towns, peaks, and landmarks are named after John Charles Frémont than any other pioneer in the history of the West!

NEW ALMADEN AND RANCHO RINCON DE SAN FRANCISQUITO

M ost, if not all, of Santa Clara County's famous **New Almaden** mine was located on the San Vincente and Canada de los Capitancillos ranchos. **Rancho Rincon de San Francisquito** is also in Santa Clara County. It was first granted to Jose Pena in 1841. The original grant was for approximately 8,418 acres. The name means the "Corner (or Bend) of the little Saint Francis."

A Fabulous Mine and a Treasure of Another Kind

I began the last chapter by remarking how one story in history often leads to another. This chapter is another example. The tale of John Charles Frémont and the Las Mariposas rancho led us to the subject of gold and the riches that have come from mines. This chapter, too, features a connection between ranchos and a money-making mine. Even though it wasn't a gold mine, it *was* one of the most famous mines in all of California history.

The story begins in the long-ago year of 1824 with a young man of Spanish descent named Secundino Robles.

The talented Secundino was an expert shot and a much-admired hunter of grizzly bears. In time, though, he would have another claim to fame. For it was Secundino who uncovered a source of great riches in the Santa Clara Valley.

In a way, the credit for the young Spaniard's discovery really belongs to some California Indians who lived in the area. It was these natives of the valley who told Secundino about a place in the nearby hills that contained red earth.

Secundino may have been the first non-Indian to learn about the strange red ore, but the Indians themselves had known about it for countless years. Old reports say that they prized it so much that they even fought wars over it. In fact, Indians from as far away as Oregon are said to have come to the Santa Clara area to obtain it.

The Indians used the red earth mostly for decoration. Among the things they decorated were their bodies. This didn't always work out for the best, for the earth contained a poison that irritated the skin and caused other problems. Because the stuff could make them sick, some old-time Indians believed that the place where they got the ore was the home of evil spirits.

When the Indians showed the red earth to Secundino Robles, he thought it presented other possibilities besides decoration. Along with his brother, Teodoro, and a couple of other individuals, he carefully examined the ore. Thinking it might contain gold or silver, Secundino and his partners decided to mine it.

So it was that these men established the first mine to be worked in the area. It became known as La Mina Santa Clara (The

Mine of Santa Clara). Unfortunately for the Robles brothers and their partners, they never found the bonanza they hoped for. After a while the mine was closed. For many years the true secret of its riches remained hidden.

In 1842 Governor Juan Bautista Alvarado granted portions of the property that contained the red earth to two individuals. These grants became known as Rancho Canada de los Capitancillos and Rancho San Vincente. In time these locations would become better known as the site of the fabulous New Almaden mine.

The story of how this came about involves another interesting person, a man named Andres Castillero. Among other things, Castillero was an engineer, a captain in the army, and a troubleshooter for the Mexican government. In late 1845, he was in California on a mission that brings up another connection between well-known names. He was trying to buy the land that belonged to John Augustus Sutter. (You remember Sutter from the New Helvetia and Las Mariposas chapters.)

It was around this time that the Mexican government was becoming worried about the number of newcomers who were finding their way to Sutter's settlement, especially Americans. With tensions growing between the United States and Mexico, it seemed like a good idea to get control of the land. However, Castillero's attempt to buy the property failed.

While he was in California, Castillero stopped by Mission Santa Clara to visit its padre, Father Real. Working at the mission was none other than Secundino Robles. Among other things, Secundino's duties included serving as the chief steward, supplies buyer, and trader. He also supervised some of the Indians who were attached to the mission.

During Castillero's visit, Secundino and his brother, Teodoro, told him about the red ore they had tried to mine in the nearby hills. The visitor was interested in their story and wanted to see a sample of the ore. So it was that the friendly Robles brothers arranged for him to visit the aged mine. The rest, as they say, is history.

Taking some of the red earth with him, Castillero made a few crude tests. After completing the tests, he announced to those who were with him that he thought the ore might be quicksilver (also known as mercury).

Throughout the ages mercury has been used for many things. Most of us know it best today as the metallic liquid we see in the tubes of thermometers. The rise and fall of the liquid in the tube tells us what the temperature is. Mercury is poisonous, a fact that explains the Indians' troubles when they used the red earth to decorate their bodies.

The possibility of finding quicksilver was interesting enough, but Castillero had another surprise in store for the Robles brothers. Besides the mercury, he reported finding signs of gold and silver in the ore!

Thinking he might have stumbled onto something very valuable, Castillero promptly filed a formal claim to the mine. But his duties soon took him away from the area, and other men took over the task of working the site.

Before long, those who were in charge of the diggings realized that they were finding a lot more quicksilver than either gold or silver. And it was the quicksilver, or mercury, that proved to be the real treasure of the "New" Almaden mine. (The mine was named after the famous Almaden quicksilver mine in Spain.)

Luckily for the mine's owners, the demand for quicksilver grew rapidly in the years after New Almaden was established. It so happens that one of mercury's many "talents" is that it is useful in separating gold and silver from their ores. With the discovery of gold in California in 1848, and the later discovery of silver in neighboring Nevada, quicksilver became even more valuable.

The red earth of New Almaden contained so much of the handy metal that the site became one of the best-known and richest quicksilver mines in the world. Sources disagree about exactly how much all the quicksilver was worth in dollars, but you can be sure that fortunes were made from the mine.

With all of the excitement taking place around the site of Secundino Robles' old mine, you might be wondering what happened to him. Well, before leaving the area, Andres Castillero set up a partnership to own and operate the mine. Among the partners were the Robles brothers.

However, the two brothers decided that they would rather own a rancho than operate a mine. So, they traded their share of the mine to a man named Jose Pena. In return, they received all or part of his Rincon de San Francisquito rancho. This property included several thousand acres located in northern Santa Clara County (near present-day Stanford University).

Along with his wife and four children, Secundino soon settled on his portion of the land. Using money he had received from the mine, Secundino set to work enlarging the Pena adobe. When he was done, the house became one of the area's most popular gathering places. Before long the fame of the Robles family's hospitality spread beyond the local community. Travelers between San Francisco and San Jose often stopped to say hello and sometimes to stay a while.

Secundino loved people, and he treated every visitor as an honored guest.

Living in the style of old-time *Californios,* at first he wouldn't think of taking a penny for his hospitality.

Things changed, though, as too many people started taking advantage of Secundino's kindness. Once again adding to his adobe, Secundino opened a kind of roadhouse (a place for travelers to eat and sleep). Now guests had to pay for their food and drink, and to enjoy the open-air dance floor he built on the roof.

Having to spend money for their pleasures certainly didn't discourage visitors. Secundino still gave all who came a warm welcome, and in a short while the Robles rancho became one of the valley's busiest stage stations and wayside stops.

Other events that drew people to the property were a variety of rodeo-like activities that were often held there. Bull-and-bear fights also took place in an arena in front of the house.

Hunters, too, made the rancho their headquarters. From there they set out to stalk mountain lions, deer, and bear. Several kinds of fowl (birds) were also hunted, including ducks, geese, quail, and snipes.

Sadly, the good times didn't last. As the years passed, problems began to arise. Secundino was fond of gambling and perhaps trusted a few too many people. In time, like John Augustus Sutter, he found his debts piling up. To pay the money he owed, he was forced to sell some of his property. The Robles rancho began to shrink in size. (Similar things happened to several other California rancheros.)

An example of how this came to be took place one day when a circus came to San Jose. Secundino loved

the excitement of such events and wanted his whole family to share in the fun. Unfortunately, he didn't have enough money to buy tickets for everyone. Rather than leave anybody out, he borrowed the money he needed.

As it turned out, his family enjoyed the show, and it was an adventure that was long remembered. Sadly, though, poor Secundino couldn't come up with the money to pay off his loan. Instead he had to give up more than 50 acres of his land—quite a price for a day at the circus!

If you're wondering how a few tickets to the circus could cost so much, you should know that the Robles family was a little larger than most. You see, Secundino and his wife had 29 children! In addition, many of their sons and daughters were married and had children of their own. So you can understand how a Robles family outing could turn into an expensive affair!

The size of Secundino's family is only one of many things that make him special. I mentioned earlier that as a young man he was quite a hunter of grizzly bears. Other things that set him apart included his close friendship with the local Indians and his dedicated work at Mission Santa Clara.

Secundino was also a loyal *Californio* who felt strongly about the events surrounding the American conquest of California. After becoming involved in a local revolt, he was captured. Rather than surrender his sword to the victorious Americans, he broke it in two.

Certainly, as far as the history books are concerned, Secundino's biggest claim to fame is the part he played in the discovery of what became the New Almaden mine. But there is something that impresses me even more about him and his wife, Maria. They and their children were people who truly lived the customs of old California. In making their rancho a place of welcome and fun, they gave thousands of lucky travelers the chance to experience the kind of hospitality that the California ranchos were famous for long ago.

With these thoughts in mind, I want to end this chapter with a tip of my hat to a genuine treasure of rancho days—the Robles family of Rancho Rincon de San Francisquito!

RANCHO LOS LAURELES

Rancho Los Laureles is located in Monterey County. It was first granted to Jose Antonio Romero in 1835. The original grant was for approximately 6,625 acres. The rancho's name comes from the Bay Laurel trees (called *laureles* in Spanish) that grew in the area.

A Famous Visitor from the Past

Like many of California's early ranchos, Rancho Los Laureles has many stories to tell. Among these tales is one stating that this Carmel Valley location was the birthplace of Jack cheese (also called Monterey Jack). Certainly many stories could be told about a period long after rancho days, when Los Laureles became a "country camp" for guests of the world-famous Hotel Del Monte in nearby Monterey. During this time, the rancho was visited by many of the wealthiest people in the United States. Still later, the site became known for the thoroughbred horses that were raised there.

My favorite tale about Los Laureles, though, tells how the rancho was paid a surprise visit by California's most feared outlaw—24 years after he was supposedly killed in a shootout with lawmen!

As if the sudden appearance of a dead man isn't enough, there's a treasure in the story, too. According to the source of the tale, the notorious bandit returned to beautiful Carmel Valley to reclaim some loot he had buried there many years before.

The story really begins in the early 1850s, when the Gold Rush was in full swing. In those rough and ready times, a number of badmen began making themselves known. Number one on the list of bandit chiefs was a man named Joaquin Murrieta. Known and feared throughout the Gold Country and other parts of the state, Murrieta became one of the West's most famous outlaws.

Like so many other people of Gold Rush days, Murrieta came to California in search of his fortune. Along with other gold seekers from his home in Sonora, Mexico, Joaquin and his wife settled in the southern mines. (The exact location of where they made camp is unclear, but it may have been near the Calaveras County mining town of San Andreas.) There they began the task of gathering gold.

Sadly, it wasn't long before Murrieta's dream of striking it rich was interrupted by events that changed his life forever. One day his camp was attacked by a rough gang of *gringos* (newcomers, usually Americans). The intruders overpowered Joaquin and assaulted his wife.

Helpless to stop them, Murrieta could only look on in rage.

There was worse to come. In another encounter with a band of gringos, Joaquin's half-brother was killed after being falsely accused of horse stealing. These tragic events prompted Murrieta to turn to a life of crime. As he started down the outlaw trail, he vowed to get revenge on each and every gringo who had taken part in the evil deeds.

Legend states that Joaquin succeeded in "evening the score" by doing away with the gringos in a variety of ways. Word of the revenge killings soon spread throughout the Gold Country. By the time the grisly task was completed, Murrieta's name was known to prospectors and townspeople alike.

Interestingly, it wasn't only the name of Joaquin Murrieta that brought fear to the fortune hunters. About the same time, a handful of other outlaws with the first name of Joaquin were also practicing their trade in the gold fields. Because Murrieta was the best known of the bunch, he and his gang were blamed for a number of crimes they didn't commit.

When things got too hot, Joaquin and some of his followers ventured into other parts of the state. There they continued their outlaw ways. On some occasions, old accounts say, they were chased to outlying areas by angry miners and hastily organized posses.

It is one such tale that brings us to Carmel Valley. Apparently a posse from the Santa Clara area was hot on Murrieta's trail. Desperately seeking a place to hide, Joaquin made it to Mission Carmel. According to legend, a friendly mission priest helped to conceal him from his pursuers. Not only did the priest hide the bandit king, but he is said to have painted the only true likeness of him that is known to exist!

With Murrieta having stayed at the famed Carmel church, it is only natural that stories of buried bonanzas and lost bandit loot would crop up in the area. Among these tales is an account of a stash of octagonal (eight-sided) gold pieces that Joaquin supposedly hid somewhere around Carmel Valley. This treasure is said to have been stolen from a mint near the Gold Country mining town of Auburn, in Placer County. It is estimated to have been worth about $75,000.

There is much more to the story of Joaquin Murrieta, but at this point you have a pretty good idea of the kind of life he led. By 1853, he had become a marked man. With violent killings and unsolved robberies continuing to take place in and about the Gold Country, the outraged citizens of mining towns began demanding "Justice!" from their elected officials.

Realizing that things were getting out of hand, lawmakers in the state capital decided to take action to stop the flood of crime. With the approval of the governor, the legislature established a special posse called the California Rangers (also known as the California State Rangers and the California Mounted Rangers). The posse was made up of a hand-picked group of very tough men who were good with guns and horses. They were given one mission—capture or kill the "five Joaquins" (and their gangs) who were terrorizing the Mother Lode!

With Captain Harry S. Love leading the way, this determined crew soon set out in pursuit of the outlaw gangs. Even though they supposedly were hunting several "Joaquins," it was the best-known of the badmen that they really wanted—Joaquin Murrieta!

For some time the posse was frustrated by wrong turns and pursuits that led to dead ends. After searches that covered hundreds of miles, they were still coming up empty-handed.

Then the Rangers got the break they were looking for. Word reached them that a suspicious band of men were camped in a remote section of Fresno County's Cantua Canyon. Once again the lawmen set off in pursuit, hoping that this time they had Murrieta where they wanted him.

In the shootout that followed, the leader of the gang was killed, along with the man who was second in command. A quick check of the bodies brought a cheer from the saddle-weary Rangers. The bandit chief was identified as Joaquin Murrieta! If that wasn't enough to bring smiles to the Rangers' faces, the second body was an added bonus. It proved to be "Three-fingered Jack" Garcia, one of Murrieta's sidekicks and a known troublemaker.

After much rejoicing the Rangers set out for the state capital (which was then in the Solano County community of Benicia). There Captain Love and his crew collected the reward for doing away with California's most wanted outlaw. To put an end to the saga of Joaquin Murrieta,

the preserved head of the dead bandit leader was put on display in various Gold Country communities where he had been well known.

With the reward paid, the governor and state legislators breathed a huge sigh of relief. At this point you might think that the story of the famed badman would surely be over. But the celebrating was barely finished when questions and rumors began to crop up. There were whispers that Murrieta *hadn't* died in Cantua Canyon after all, and a number of people questioned whether the head displayed in the Gold Country was his. To this day, historians still debate what really happened to Joaquin Murrieta.

With the mystery of Murrieta's fate still unsolved, the tale of the strange visitor to the Los Laureles rancho takes on added meaning. The story comes from notes left by Daniel Ross Martin, a pioneer Monterey County resident who was born along the Big Sur coast in 1859.

Martin's account dates from 1877, two dozen years after Joaquin Murrieta was said to have died in a hail of gunfire. In that year Martin was working as a cowboy on Rancho Los Laureles. Early one morning he was putting on his boots when the ranch foreman, Kinzie Klinkenbeard, came by. The foreman asked Martin to hold up going to work for a while because he wanted him to witness a conversation.

Soon an older man of Spanish descent approached. The visitor asked Klinkenbeard how much he owed for his night's stay. "You don't owe anything," the foreman replied. "We're of the old California style here. Travelers are welcome, and they can stay as long as they wish."

As the conversation continued, Klinkenbeard began asking the older man some questions. Had the man ever been in the Sierra Nevada, he wondered?

"Yes," his guest answered.

Well, then, the foreman asked, had he ever stopped at Klinkenbeard's Roadhouse to buy provisions and spend the night? (The roadhouse was located between Truckee and Lake Tahoe.)

With a surprised look, the visitor nodded that he had.

"How did you know?" he asked Klinkenbeard.

Realizing he might be getting on touchy ground,

the foreman quickly explained that the roadhouse had belonged to his father. Kinzie had worked at the inn as a boy and remembered waiting on the older man and his companions when they had stayed at the inn many years before.

Then Klinkenbeard took a deep breath and asked the question he had been leading up to.

"Are you Joaquin Murrieta?"

"Yes," said the visitor.

Amazed by this matter-of-fact reply, the flustered foreman blurted, "Don't you know you are supposed to have been killed?"

"I heard so," the older man responded, "but I got away and went to Mexico. The Americans were getting too *valiente* (desperate)."

According to Daniel Ross Martin, "Murrieta" went on to explain that he had returned to the area to claim some treasure he had hidden many years earlier. (Based on the location, this treasure was apparently *not* the "takings" from the Auburn mint mentioned earlier in this chapter.) He added that he had visited the Laureles rancho in hopes of finding the Boronda family there. (Interestingly, a check of the records shows that the Boronda family *had* been there during the Murrieta reign of terror.)

Finally, before saddling his horse and taking his leave, the visitor indicated that he would soon be leaving California and heading back to Mexico to be with his people.

Martin's amazing story supports other accounts that have cast doubt on whether Joaquin Murrieta really died in 1853. But if the bandit chief *wasn't* killed by Captain Love and his men in Cantua Canyon, whose head was put on display after the shootout?

One idea comes from a respected California historian named Frank F. Latta. Before he died, Latta spent more than half a century researching the life of Murrieta. He believed that the mysterious head may have belonged to an Indian by the name of Chappo, who worked for the Murrieta gang as a hostler (someone who takes care of horses). Incidentally, Chappo was originally from Carmel Valley.

It's only fair to tell you that people still disagree about when and how Murrieta may have met his end. In fact, so many legends have grown up around the famed outlaw that some historians have even doubted whether there ever *was* a Joaquin Murrieta! I, for one, believe that Daniel Ross Martin *did* see the real Murrieta in 1877. I also believe that the former outlaw returned to Mexico after leaving the Los Laureles rancho—and *after* he recovered a long-buried treasure!

You see, legend has it that a few days after the mysterious visitor rode off into the hills, a freshly dug hole was found. At the bottom of the hole was the rusted imprint of an aged metal cauldron (pot). What was in the pot, only the finder knows. But we can make a pretty good guess, and most of those who know the story of Joaquin's "return from the dead" would agree.

These people think that the rusty pot was filled with bandit loot. They also believe that it was carried back to Mexico by a legendary badman—a man who had supposedly been killed by the California Rangers 24 years before!

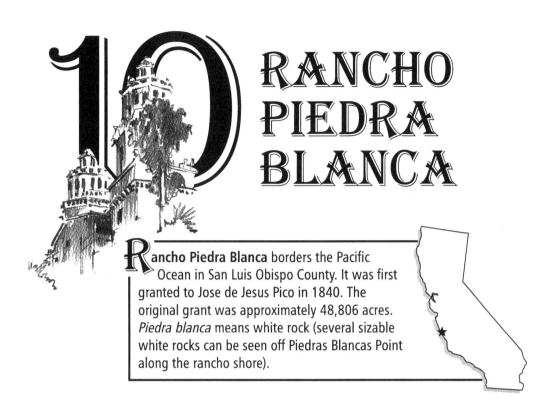

10 RANCHO PIEDRA BLANCA

Rancho Piedra Blanca borders the Pacific Ocean in San Luis Obispo County. It was first granted to Jose de Jesus Pico in 1840. The original grant was approximately 48,806 acres. *Piedra blanca* means white rock (several sizable white rocks can be seen off Piedras Blancas Point along the rancho shore).

A Castle for California

Our final chapter takes us to the beautiful coastline of San Luis Obispo County. As you will see, this land of green hills and crashing waves is a fitting place to end our collection of rancho stories. Besides the countless *tales* connected with the area, it became the site of one of the greatest collections of *treasures* in the world. In fact, so rich is this hoard of priceless objects that no one can even guess how much it is worth!

Before I get to this fabulous treasure, I want to mention our old friend John Charles Frémont. (You probably remember meeting Frémont in the New Helvetia and Las Mariposas chapters.) The famed Pathfinder played a brief but important part in the life of the original owner of the property.

The story concerns Jose de Jesus Pico, who was granted Rancho Piedra Blanca in 1840. During the fight for control of California later in the 1840s, Pico was arrested by Frémont. Sources differ about what crime he was charged with, but most agree that he was condemned to death.

Before Pico could face the firing squad, a band of weeping women and children gathered together and pleaded with the Pathfinder to let him live. (They may have included members of Pico's own family.) Moved by their pleas, Frémont is reported to have said, "I can fight men but I cannot fight women—I give you his life."

In turn, the pardoned Mr. Pico became one of Frémont's most devoted friends. Later he assisted the American soldier in bringing about the treaty of Cahuenga. As you may remember, this treaty officially ended the war between the Mexican and American forces in California.

It was on part of Pico's Piedra Blanca property that a little town grew up that was called San Simeon (in honor of Saint Simon). This village was nestled on San Simeon Point, which curves around a small natural harbor known as San Simeon Bay.

In the days before the ranchos, this stretch of coastline was known to Indians and Spanish explorers. During the Mission Period, the padres were familiar with it as well. In fact, Mission San Miguel's land once included much of this area. Among other things, the mission padres used the coastal land for farming and for grazing herds of cattle and horses.

It wasn't until the 1850s or 1860s, though, that the settlement of San Simeon really came into its own. During this period, whalers (whale hunters) developed the village and its harbor into a port for their activities.

The type of whaling done at San Simeon was known as shore whaling. Whalers killed the great creatures at sea and then towed the carcasses to the shore, where they were processed. The most valuable product gained from the whales was oil, which in those days was the main fuel for lamps.

In 1865 a new chapter began in the story of San Simeon. In that year a wealthy man by the name of George Hearst purchased much of the property in the area. Hearst had come to California during the Gold Rush. Although he didn't get rich in the gold fields, his luck changed with the silver strike in Nevada some years later.

Perhaps it was Hearst's interest in mining that prompted him to buy the land. It seems that cinnabar (the ore of mercury, or quicksilver) had been discovered in the Santa Lucia mountain range, east of San Simeon. In the early 1860s, word of the discovery spread throughout many of the mining districts in California and Nevada. Hundreds of miners flocked to the region, but the man who bought the property was George Hearst.

As it turned out, the cinnabar deposits were small compared to those at the rich New Almaden mine in Santa Clara County (which you may remember from Chapter 8). But Hearst didn't give up on the land. Instead, he encouraged the whalers to continue their trade. Meanwhile, he spent both time and money developing the property. Among other things, he constructed a large ranch house behind the whaling village.

In 1878 Hearst built a 1,000-foot wharf at the harbor. The wharf

boasted a horse-drawn railroad to help with the loading and unloading of ships. To give you some idea of the activities that were taking place in the area, let me list some of the items that were shipped from the port of San Simeon during the wharf's first year of operation.

As you might expect, one local product was mercury from the cinnabar mines. But visiting ships also picked up butter, eggs, chickens, tallow, beef, hides, and wool. Crops such as wheat, barley, and oats traveled down the wharf and onto the vessels, along with dried seaweed and abalone (a kind of shellfish that was prized for its meat and shell). By the way, the abalone and seaweed were harvested by Chinese workers along the coast in the northern part of the county.

On the shore of San Simeon Bay, Hearst also built a warehouse that measured 4,800 square feet. It was said to be one of the finest such structures on the entire Pacific Coast.

George Hearst's improvements helped to make San Simeon known to many people, but it was his son, William Randolph Hearst, who made the area famous around the world. The younger Hearst loved the beauty of the land that was once Rancho Piedra Blanca. And it was on the grounds of the old rancho that he found the ideal place to build the "country home" of his dreams.

The site was on a hilltop that overlooked the Pacific Ocean and the coastal mountain range. In time, because of William Randolph Hearst, this location came to be known as the Enchanted Hill.

What made the hilltop so magical? Well, when William Randolph Hearst set out to do something, he did it in a big way. Beginning in 1919, he began building his "country home," and he continued adding to it for nearly 30 years. By the time he was done, he had created a magnificent palace and filled it with priceless treasures from around the world. Known today as Hearst Castle, it became a gathering place for the rich and famous, including United States presidents, movie stars, and many other celebrities.

Before I tell you more about the castle and its grounds, I want to mention the person who designed it. What makes this talented individual even more special is that *she* was something of a pioneer, for in those years architects were almost always men. The name of this San Francisco-born architect was Julia Morgan. Thanks to Hearst Castle, it was a name that became known around the world.

A number of impressive structures were built on the Hearst estate, but the main house alone was a fantastic place. To give you some idea of just how special this

"mountain-top monument" was, let's take a peek inside a couple of the rooms as they looked when Hearst welcomed visitors to his castle.

We'll begin with the huge room known as the Assembly Hall. Like the rest of the great house, the hall was constructed of materials that Hearst brought to San Simeon Bay from around the world. Its walls were made of aged ivory. Lining the walls were hand-carved choir stalls that came from old churches in Italy. Above the stalls were colorful tapestries (hand-woven wall hangings) that once belonged to the royal family of Spain. Huge tapestries also hung above the wide windows at each end of the room.

The room's immense fireplace was about 400 years old. It was imported from France and then installed in the Assembly Hall. Also impressive were the carved tables, striking statues, ornate candelabras, elegant rugs, and priceless antiques that decorated the hall.

Even with all of these rare and one-of-a-kind items, my favorite feature of all was one that most visitors never even saw. Hidden behind a secret panel was a carved wooden elevator. Each evening at 7:30, Mr. Hearst would exit this private elevator to greet his dinner guests.

The mention of dinner brings me to the second room I want to tell you about, the castle's Dining Hall. This room was said to be one of Hearst's favorites. Like the Assembly Hall (and other rooms in the palace), it contained an almost unbelievable collection of antique treasures.

To me, one of the most impressive of the Dining Hall's features was its ceiling. This carved masterpiece was centuries old. It had been found in an ancient Italian monastery (a place where a religious community of men called monks lived). Like the Assembly Hall, the room was lined with antique choir stalls, which came from a cathedral in Spain. To keep up the church theme of the ceiling and choir stalls, larger-than-life sculptured figures of saints were placed in niches about the room.

Also visible on the side walls were carved body rests, where knights of old rested their heavy armor centuries ago. The centerpiece of the room, of course, was the dining table, a massive piece accompanied by matching chairs. At one end of the room was another huge fireplace, which was big enough for a tall man to walk into. It came from a historic building in France.

Adding color to the room were two large antique tapestries. High above them and the choir stalls, festive banners were hung, each portraying the crest of an Italian noble family. If you imagine this impressive room aglow with the flickering light of the great fireplace and dozens of candles, you can get some idea of the special place it became when guests came to dine.

It wasn't only the buildings and their furnishings that made Hearst's country estate so remarkable. The grounds surrounding the castle and other structures were equally impressive. Guests enjoyed strolling through the glorious gardens, which contained trees and plants from around the world that were always in bloom.

On the ocean side of the hill, there was a breath-taking swimming pool made of prized Italian marble and surrounded by ancient Roman and Greek statues. This immense pool was big enough to float a large boat in! At one end, Hearst placed a bath house for the convenience of his guests—not just any old bath house, of course, but one he imported specially from Greece.

If Hearst's guests didn't care to swim, they could play tennis on a pair of courts located on the inland side of the hill, or they could use the fancy gym nearby. If they liked their swimming indoors, they could use a second swimming pool. This one was 84 feet long and 40 feet wide, and it had a smaller pool next to it for children.

The huge room that contained the indoor pools took Italian craftsmen nearly three and a half years to build. It featured thousands of pieces of gold-leaf marble tile and Venetian glass. The water for the pools was pumped from the Pacific Ocean (more than six miles away), just so Hearst's guests could experience the thrill of swimming in ocean water without having to brave wind, waves, or fog!

As if all this wasn't spectacular enough, the Enchanted Hill had another unusual feature as well. Some visitors found it the most fascinating of all. (I imagine that children especially liked it.) At one time the estate housed what was said to be the largest private zoo in the world!

The zoo boasted caged creatures from such faraway places as Africa and India. Other animals had their own areas in which to roam. They included elk, bison, llamas, zebras, giraffes, camels, antelope, and kangaroos. There was also a large collection of members of the cat family—wildcats, cheetahs, leopards, lions, and even a rare black panther. The bear family was also represented, including the white polar bear of the Arctic and the black bear of Alaska.

Monkeys of many kinds were a special hit with visitors, not to mention a hairy orangutang (a member of the ape family). And what is a zoo without an elephant?

So you can see why the hilltop, with its fairy-tale castle and its collection of animals, might become known as the Enchanted Hill. Yet this large estate was only a small part of the land held by William Randolph Hearst. In time he outdid the rancheros of old by buying more property in both San Luis Obispo and Monterey counties.

At one time these holdings stretched up and down the coast a distance of approximately 50 miles, and pushed inland to include almost a quarter of a million acres! (That's about five times the size of Jose de Jesus Pico's original grant.)

William Randolph Hearst died in 1951. Seven years later, the Hearst Corporation gave his great castle (along with about 125 acres of surrounding land) to the State of California. The gift of this kingly domain means that its treasures now belong to the people of California, and they are waiting there for you to see.

If you do visit this magical place, let me ask one small favor. As you step away from the Enchanted Hill, look to the north. There you will see miles of rolling green hills and uncluttered beaches. Because this wonderland of beauty is still unspoiled, you will be seeing a scene similar to what Jose de Jesus Pico saw when he gazed out upon his Piedra Blanca grant more than a century and a half ago. Imagine

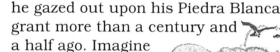

yourself as a member of a ranchero's family, and pause a moment to see the land as they did, full of beauty and promise, a place to enjoy and to cherish.

We can't bring back those days of old, but we *can* remember that many of California's special places were once part of its vast rancho system. I've told you about several of them in this book, but there are lots more to discover—along with the tales and treasures that are so much a part of the colorful heritage of the Golden State!

AUTHOR'S NOTES

As with other books in the **History & Happenings of California Series,** this Author's Notes section provides additional information about many of the **people, places,** and **events** mentioned in the text. Of course, no book of this size could tell the whole story of California's ranchos, but these Notes may suggest some starting points for doing your own research into topics that interest you.

Before I begin, I want to extend my heartfelt thanks to Bob Reese, former historian for the California State Department of Parks and Recreation. Bob read an early draft of Part One of this book for historical accuracy and made several helpful suggestions.

Part One introduces **"rancho days,"** a time that some have described as a Golden Age. As I hinted in the first chapter, this period does not have exact boundaries. Perhaps it is safest to say that it began in the mid-1820s and lasted until 1846, the year of the American conquest of California. Of course, there were ranchos dating back to Spanish times, and some ranchos lasted even into the 20th century. However, it was during the time of Mexican rule that the ranchos enjoyed their greatest prosperity.

Some numbers may help make the picture a little clearer. During the more than 50 years that Spain was in control of California, fewer than 25 ranchos were established. After Mexico gained its independence, more than

600 grants were given in less than half that period of time. The great majority of these grants were made between 1834 and 1846, when Mexican rule came to an end.

A key event in defining the rancho period was the passage of the Secularization Act by the Mexican Congress in 1833 (some sources say 1834). This act was influenced by Mexico's disapproval of the way the old Spanish missions were being run. In part the law forced the church to give up much of its land, opening up thousands of acres of prized property. The legislation was an important reason that the ranchos became the main economic and social institutions in Alta California.

For some fortunate landowners, rancho days may indeed have been a Golden Age. But for many **California Indians,** it was a time of disappointment. As the church gave up much of its land, the padres were unable to care for the mission Indians in the way they had before. This created confusion and hardship for many of those who had learned to look to the church for guidance, shelter, and food.

As I mention in the text, half of the old mission land was supposed to go to the Indians who had worked it. Unfortunately, even though some native Californians did obtain land, many others lost their claims through being talked or cheated out of them.

To see the role of the mission lands in establishing the rancho period, you might try comparing a map of the old church properties with one of California's ranchos. The comparison would show that the missions and ranchos were often located in the same general areas, stretching up and down the central and southern California coasts. The ranchos, however, often extended farther inland than the mission properties and reached higher up into northern California. There were also some outlying ranchos surrounded by large areas of unclaimed land.

When land grants were given, the property was measured in leagues. One square league was a little more than 4,438 acres, which would be considered a good-sized ranch today. In fact, though, one square league was usually the *minimum* amount of land that was granted! The *maximum* for a single grant was 11 square leagues, which amounted to more than 48,000 acres, or 75 square miles!

In addition, there was no limit to the number of people in a family who could obtain a grant, as long as they qualified and were approved by the authorities. As a result, some families accumulated huge tracts of land. For example, the de la Guerra family of southern California was able to acquire 14 claims through a combination of grants and purchases of property. These claims added up to more than 480,000 acres, or 750 square miles!

Of course, the land was valuable mostly to the extent that it could be profitably worked, particularly to raise cattle for the **hide and tallow trade.** This trade was the basis of the ranchos' prosperity. For this reason it would be hard to overestimate how important the trading ships, or **Boston traders,** were for the lifestyle enjoyed by the rancheros.

Under Spanish rule, many of the trade ship captains were forced to do their business secretly ("by the light of the moon"), because Spain forbade trade with individuals from other lands. After Mexico freed itself from Spain, the laws were changed to allow trade with other nations, including the United States.

It was from the trading vessels that rancheros acquired many useful items as well as the kinds of luxuries mentioned in Chapter 1. By the way, the quotation describing the cargo of the trading ship ***Pilgrim*** is taken from the famous book *Two Years Before the Mast,* by Richard H. Dana, Jr.

The "money" the rancheros used to acquire these goods consisted of the hides of cattle as well as the tallow made from the animals' fat. It was for this reason that cattle hides became known as **California bank notes.**

They were also sometimes referred to as "leather dollars." Usually a single hide was worth somewhere between one and three American dollars, while 25 pounds of tallow was worth about $1.50.

Although hides and tallow were the most sought-after items taken from the cattle, sometimes part of the animal's meat was cut into strips and dried so it could be eaten later. In addition, the untanned skin of the cattle (rawhide) was often in demand. Described as a general repair-all, rawhide was also used to make such things as *reatas* (lariats or ropes), bridle reins, lashings, bedsprings, chair bottoms, and floor mats.

Chapter 2 provides additional detail about the lifestyle based on cattle raising and the hide and tallow trade. This way of life began to decline with the American takeover of California and the advent of the Gold Rush a few years later. But even though rancho days represented a relatively short period of time, they played a colorful and important part in California history.

After the introduction provided by the first two chapters, Part Two takes readers to a number of rancho locations around the Golden State. The remainder of these Notes provide some additional details about these properties and the **tales and treasures** connected with them.

Rancho La Brea (Chapter 3) was originally part of the Los Angeles pueblo. Today the famous **La Brea "tar pits"** are surrounded by the sprawling city.

As stated in the text, California Indians from throughout the area (mainly the Chumash and Gabrielinos) used the tar-like goo from the La Brea deposits for waterproofing their boats, among other things. The boats in question at this early time were often a kind of "plank canoe" that was used along the coast, often to visit offshore islands. Other uses the Indians found for the tar included mending broken implements, securing handles to knives and other tools, and fastening shells and other colorful objects to ceremonial pieces and household items.

As strange as it seems, California's **"black gold"** (which is also referred to as "rock oil" and petroleum) is classified as a mineral, along with such things as gold, silver, and coal. Of all California's minerals, oil has brought the greatest wealth to the Golden State.

Today the La Brea deposits are part of Hancock Park. The park is named after George Allen Hancock, who donated the land on which it is located and contributed to the successful preservation of the fossils. Except for the actual pits themselves, perhaps the highlight of the park is the George C. Page Museum, which houses the Rancho La Brea collection of fossilized plants and animals. (It was Page who provided the funds to build the museum.)

The Page Museum is part of the Natural History Museum of Los Angeles. It is located near the Los Angeles County Museum of Art (which is also at Hancock Park). Hancock Park is on Wilshire Boulevard, between Ogden and Curson Streets, approximately seven miles west of the Los Angeles civic center.

There is some uncertainty about the circumstances surrounding the grant of **El Refugio** (Chapter 4). Most of my sources indicate that **Jose Francisco Ortega** was granted the El Refugio property in the mid-1790s (probably 1795). Others say that he couldn't have been given "title" to the land at that time, because Spanish law stated that it was being held "in trust" for the Indians. However, it is known that the Ortega family moved onto the property prior to the 1800s—legally or not—and remained there for many years. In the early 1830s (when the missions were being secularized, and more than a decade after Mexico had gained its independence from Spain) the Ortega family still occupied El Refugio. It was at this time that more than 26,500 acres were officially "regranted" to one of Jose Francisco Ortega's descendants.

Unfortunately, Jose Francisco, the original grant holder, wasn't able to enjoy his rancho for very long. He died of a heart attack in 1798 while he was on his way to the Santa Barbara presidio to see his son.

The description of the **earthquake and tidal wave of December 21, 1812,** as the worst such events ever to have been recorded in the Santa Barbara area comes from *It Happened in Old Santa Barbara,* a book written by well-known Santa Barbara historian Walker A. Tompkins. The earthquakes of December 1812 are well known for damaging the missions of La Purisima, Santa Ines, San Fernando, San Juan Capistrano, San Gabriel, and Santa Barbara. Incidentally, in reading about the missions and mission communities, you may discover that **Santa Ines** is also spelled "Inez" and "Ynez."

Besides damage to buildings, the earthquakes of December 1812 also caused a number of "smoke-belching sulphur volcanos" to erupt from the ground. Many of these mini-volcanos were in the Santa Barbara area, with one of them even erupting on the beach!

With the mention of beaches, I'm reminded that at one time El Refugio beach (or, to be more accurate, all of **Refugio Bay**) was considered a smuggler's haven. In fact, this secluded cove has been described as the chief *contrabandista* (smuggling) port on the California coast. Among the items that were brought to this bay for barter were food, furniture, medicines, dry goods, and tools. These were traded for such things as hides, tallow, leather goods, and wine.

Speaking of illegal activities associated with the sea brings to mind **Hippolyte de Bouchard.** For simplicity's sake, I refer to him as a "pirate" in the text, but whether he was a pirate (acting completely on his own, as an outlaw) or a privateer (authorized by a government) has been debated for so long, and in so many sources, that I will leave it up to you to decide for yourself. Bouchard did sail under the flag of the Republic of Buenos Aires, which seems to make him a privateer. However, when we consider the way he attacked and sacked California's capital city of Monterey, the term *pirate* also seems appropriate. Maybe he was a little bit of both.

Much of the El Refugio chapter centers on the exploits of **Joseph Chapman,** a truly remarkable pioneer of rancho days. Among the sources who indicate that the unwilling pirate escaped from Bouchard at El Refugio (and not in Monterey) was a descendant of Joseph Chapman whom I was able to track down. The summary description of Chapman quoted in the text comes from the noted California historian Hubert Howe Bancroft, not a man to give out praise lightly.

The next chapter, on **Rancho San Joaquin** (Chapter 5), begins by following Hippolyte de Bouchard to the area around **San Juan Capistrano** and **Rancho Trabuco.** With stories of lost and found treasures being a colorful part of this region's lore, a tale about another kind of "treasure" might also be of interest. This account goes back to 1769, when the Gaspar de Portola expedition ventured up the California coast in search of Monterey Bay. As the story goes, when the expedition crossed the land that was to become Rancho Trabuco, one of the soldiers lost a type of gun known as a blunderbuss (a kind of forerunner of the shotgun). Interestingly, *trabuco* is Spanish for blunderbuss, which helps to explain how this area got its name. As to the lost weapon, wouldn't it be nice to find the remains of the gun? This, to me, would be a *treasure* money can't buy.

Before leaving Bouchard and his visit to San Juan, I would like to mention that **Dana's Cove** (where he dropped anchor) gained its name from Richard Henry Dana. In the mid-1830s Dana worked as a sailor aboard the *Pilgrim*, the trading ship mentioned in Chapter 1. His popular book *Two Years Before the Mast* contains a delightful description of the same small bay that had sheltered Bouchard in 1818, as well as the activities that went on there. Anyone interested in "Boston traders" and

California's early hide and tallow trade will find the book fascinating.

In regard to **Andres Sepulveda** and the handsome adobe house he named Refugio, some sources say the striking structure *wasn't* on Rancho San Joaquin. However, the highly respected book *A Companion to California,* by James D. Hart, does locate the "great house" on Sepulveda's San Joaquin grant.

Accounts of the famous and thrilling race between Sepulveda's prized **Black Swan** and Pio Pico's **Sarco** differ in detail. Among other things, there are conflicting reports as to whether the $25,000 wager between Sepulveda and Pico was in gold, as I state in the text, or cash. Either way, it was a gigantic bet then—and it would be even bigger now! Descriptions of the race itself also differ in some ways. However, on one thing all accounts agree: Black Swan was the winner!

The word "gigantic" might also be applied to the **Irvine Ranch.** Information from the Irvine Company states that the original Irvine Ranch amounted to approximately 120,000 acres (almost 200 square miles)! This huge chunk of land was about eight miles wide and extended more than 21 miles inland from the sea. Much of this land is now developed, and privately owned. Among many other developments, the property boasts the community of **Irvine,** which was incorporated as a city in 1971. One of Irvine's claims to fame is its distinction of having been the largest master-planned urban community in the United States.

In reading about **John Augustus Sutter** and **New Helvetia** (Chapter 6), you might have wondered why **Governor Alvarado** was so eager to help the Swiss fugitive with his plan to settle in the Sacramento Valley. Among other things, Alvarado hoped that Sutter's settlement would serve as a buffer between the outlying Mexican ranchos and certain groups of "hostile" Indians. He also thought that Sutter's presence would help check the power and influence of his uncle and rival, **Mariano Guadalupe Vallejo.**

Beginning with the establishment of **Sutter's Fort,** the former Swiss pauper went on to become one of the greatest landowners in all of California. The size of his original grant was comparable to a number of other ranchos, but in 1841 the busy Mr. Sutter also acquired **Fort Ross** (located along the rugged California coast, north of Bodega Bay). Then, in 1845, **Governor Manuel Micheltorena** rewarded Sutter for supplying him with military aid by giving him even more land. The Micheltorena grant is reported to have been twice the size of Sutter's original holdings. One respected source stated that, taken together, Sutter's holdings were perhaps as big as any ever privately assembled in the United States! Of course, in the end Sutter lost much of his "kingdom," including the huge Micheltorena grant (which was denied him by decisions of the United States Supreme Court).

Interestingly, even though Sutter at one time owned a huge chunk of land, sources differ on whether the site of the sawmill built by **James Wilson Marshall** was part of it. The area along the South Fork of the American River where the mill was built was called Cul-huh-mah by the Indians. Today this location is known as Coloma. (Incidentally, there are various spellings for the original name, including Cullomah, Culloma, and Culluma.)

The mill site (along with over 100 additional acres along El Dorado County's historic Highway 49) is now part of the California State Park System, as is Sutter's restored fort. Both are registered historical landmarks and well worth a visit.

As with Coloma, the name of Sutter's **Hock Farm** may also be Indian in origin. Some sources indicate that the word "hock" is an Indian word, and one source goes so far as to say that Sutter named his Feather River farm after a large Indian village in the area.

Speaking of names, over a period of years I have spent a good deal of time trying to settle the question of what Sutter called his pet bulldog. Other than **Beppo** (which may have been short for Beppino), I have found the names Brave and Burgy in reference to it. Having owned three English bulldogs in my life, I felt Beppo was the most fitting and chose to use it in my retelling.

I must confess that we can't be sure the animal was an *English* bulldog. At least one source specifies this breed, but most accounts refer to Beppo simply as a bulldog. To add to the confusion, one source states the animal was a large mastiff, and another hints that it may have been a mongrel-like sheepdog. While I am partial to the English bulldog theory, we can be sure that, whatever the breed, Beppo was one historic dog!

In introducing **Las Mariposas** (Chapter 7), I mention the man credited with the name Mariposa, **Gabriel Moraga.** According to historian James D. Hart, Moraga originated several other California place names as well, including Calaveras, Merced, Sacramento, and San Joaquin. He also was responsible for opening trade with the Russians at Fort Ross (the outpost later acquired by none other than John Augustus Sutter).

Interestingly, Gabriel's son Joaquin became a ranchero in what is now Contra Costa County. The valley and town of Moraga (site of St. Mary's College) are named for him.

Speaking of names, most historians are partial to the idea that the name Mariposa originated with the Gabriel Moraga expedition and its encounter with thousands of butterflies. (As you probably recall, *mariposa* is Spanish for butterfly.) One source even states that the butterflies were so thick that one "had to be extricated from a soldier's ear." I should note, though, that there are a couple of other theories as to how the name Mariposa originated. One tale states that it was taken from "Mariposa Lily," a relatively common name for the multicolored lilies that grow in the region in late spring and early summer. Another suggests that the name was taken from the thousands of butterfly-like poppies that dotted the nearby hills.

In this chapter, as is the case with many of the ranchos, the story of the owners is as colorful as the story of the land. Certainly this is true of Rancho Las Mariposas, which became the property of **John Charles Frémont** and his wife, **Jessie.**

Of course, the Pathfinder had already made quite a name for himself before acquiring the gold-laden rancho (even if he did have the help of such renowned mountain men as **Kit Carson** and **Joseph Walker**). During the period of the American takeover of California, Frémont seems to have been busy stirring up a good deal of trouble. It was after being asked to leave the Monterey area that Frémont surprised the Mexican authorities by raising an American flag over a log fort atop **Hawk's Peak.** Most sources agree that the flag in question was the Stars and Stripes, but a handful suggest that it was the banner of the U.S. Army Corps of Engineers. Either way, some historians see this incident as "the first open act of hostility" in the conquest of California. A California State Historical Landmark commemorating the event is located in San Juan Bautista's Abbey Park (on the southeast corner of Fourth and Muckelem streets).

Incidentally, other than Hawk's Peak and Frémont Peak, the site of the fort was also known as Gabilan (Gavilan) Peak. (The name means sparrow hawk in Spanish.)

In reference to Frémont's acceptance of the Mexican surrender in California (January 13, 1847), this historic event took place at the **Cahuenga** adobe, near the entrance of Cahuenga Pass (Los Angeles County). A California State Historical Landmark honoring this event can be seen at 3919 Lankershim Boulevard in North Hollywood.

As I hinted in the text, John Charles Frémont has been the subject of a good deal of controversy and mixed judgments over the years. Certainly, the way he stretched the boundaries of his Mariposa grant to include mines and land that were already being worked by others is questionable at best. But we also need to remember that the courts eventually confirmed his property lines.

Interestingly, according to several sources the agent who bought the "wrong" property for Frémont was the respected Thomas Oliver Larkin, a former United States consul, confidential agent of the government, and successful businessman. It's hard to imagine such an apparently upright citizen purposely taking Frémont's money and purchasing several thousand acres of "worthless" land many miles from where Frémont wanted to be. However, every once in a while I come across an account that indicates it was none other than Larkin who ended up with the property Frémont originally wanted! If this is true, it may help to explain how the Pathfinder ended up with his foothill land.

As for how much gold came out of Frémont's Mariposa grant, it is estimated to have been worth approximately $10 million in 1859! Considering that Larkin acquired the property for a mere $3,000, I think it's safe to say that the purchase was truly a "golden" mistake!

With all of this wealth, why was Frémont nearly broke when he died? One reason was that after selling Las Mariposas he invested, unwisely, in a variety of schemes, mainly western railroad projects.

As for the brave and talented Jessie Frémont, she deserves a chapter all to herself. Better yet, you might want to look up her own writings in such works as *The Story of the Guard, Far-West Sketches,* and *The Will and the Way Stories.*

The story of the **New Almaden Mine** (Chapter 8) is one of the most interesting in California history, and its tangled court cases and controversies are discussed to this day by historians. Most or all of the mine's workings were located on two Santa Clara Valley ranchos. The first, Rancho San Vincente, was originally granted in 1842 to Jose de los Reyes Berreyesa (also spelled Berryessa and Berryesa). The original grant was for approximately 4,438 acres. San Vincente honors Saint Vincent. The second, Rancho Canada de los Capitancillos, was granted to Justo Larios, also in 1842. Sources disagree as to its original size, with most listings indicating it was between 3,360 and 4,470 acres. There is also confusion as to the meaning of the name. Perhaps "The Glen (or Valley) of the Little Captains" is the most accurate, as some early Californians are said to have referred to some of the local Indians as "Little Captains."

The **red earth** that contained New Almaden's **quicksilver** is sometimes called cinnabar. Cinnabar is the most important ore of quicksilver, or mercury. The Indian word for the red earth was *mohetka.*

Just how valuable was New Almaden's quicksilver? In 1945 State Mineralogist Walter M. Bradley estimated that the mine had already produced quicksilver worth $70 million—and it continued to operate until the 1970s! Whatever the exact total may be, New Almaden proved to be the most important mercury mine in the United States—and the single most profitable mine of any kind in the history of California! History buffs may wish to note that the Guadalupe—a second profitable quicksilver mine—was also developed in the area.

As I related in the text, it was **Andres Castillero** who conducted the tests that led to renewed mining at the New Almaden site. Castillero may have had more than one reason for being in California around this time. Besides attempting to buy John Augustus Sutter's land, he is also said to have been working on a plan to bring additional Mexican troops into the area to help control the foreigners who were flocking to California in ever-increasing numbers.

By the way, **Father Real,** whom Castillero stopped at Mission Santa Clara to visit, is said to have been a cousin of **Secundino and Teodoro Robles.** Along with the Robles brothers, he was also one of the participants in the partnership Castillero set up to own and operate the mine.

Much of what I learned about **Rancho Los Laureles** (Chapter 9) has come from talking to old-timers. Their colorful accounts—tales, legends, anecdotes, and memories—often are far more fascinating than the history recounted in books.

Anyone can do this kind of research, and you never know when you'll strike "gold," as I did with the tale of the return of **Joaquin Murrieta** to Carmel Valley. Pioneer Monterey County resident **Daniel Ross Martin** was my primary source for this story. Interestingly, if Martin's family hadn't encouraged him to jot down some of the things he remembered most from his long and eventful life, his description of Joaquin's return to the Laureles rancho might never have been recorded. This example shows how important it is for people like you and me to track down and record the tales the old-timers have to tell while they are still able to relate them.

Incidentally, there were actually two neighboring ranchos in Carmel Valley that were known by the name of Los Laureles. The smaller of the two consisted of less than 1,000 acres, making it one of the smallest ranchos in Monterey County.

It was on the larger of the two ranchos that Daniel Ross Martin met the man who claimed to be Joaquin Murrieta. In recounting this incident, I used a certain "author's license" to re-create the scene and the conversation. However, the facts are as reported in the Martin account.

In case you're interested in hunting for the **buried pot of octagonal gold pieces** that Murrieta supposedly buried in the Carmel Valley area, I should note that it may contain somewhat less than the $75,000 taken from the

Auburn mint. Aged reports say that at least $10,000 of the loot was recovered in the years following the robbery. As a further caution, tales of treasures like this one (as well as the **metal cauldron** mentioned at the end of the chapter) often turn out to be more fiction than fact. But then again, you never know!

A treasure of another kind is the **portrait of Joaquin Murrieta** that was supposed to have been painted by a Carmel Mission priest. The painting is reported to be in a private collection in southern California.

While some have questioned whether Joaquin Murrieta was a real historical figure, there doesn't seem to have been any doubt on the part of the lawmakers of the day. The **California Rangers** were established by an act of the California legislature on May 17, 1853, for the expressed purpose of "capturing the party or gang of robbers commanded by the five Joaquins." Prominent on the list was Joaquin Murrieta (spelled "Muriati" in the legislation).

The exact location of the famed **California Ranger–Murrieta gang shootout** is difficult to pinpoint, but several sources suggest it took place in the **Cantua Canyon** area of west Fresno County, near Murrieta Springs. A California Historical Landmark commemorating the event is on State Highway 198, approximately nine miles north of the community of Coalinga.

Inasmuch as historian **Frank F. Latta** suggested another identity for the head that was displayed after the shootout, it should come as no surprise that he was of the opinion that Joaquin Murrieta was *not* killed in Cantua Canyon. If you've been "hooked" by the Murrieta story, you might want to track down a copy of Latta's informative book *Joaquin Murrieta and His Horse Gangs*.

Chapter 10 tells the story of California's own castle, built on land that was once part of **Rancho Piedra Blanca.** The original ranchero, **Jose de Jesus Pico,** was a cousin of Pio Pico, the last governor of Mexican California.

The former Pico went on to become something of a legend in San Luis Obispo County. He was also closely associated with Mission San Miguel (east of his rancho), and it is to him that colorful accounts of a secret gold mine near Mission San Luis Obispo can be traced. Speaking of gold, Pico himself was bitten by the gold bug, and made successful trips to California's Gold Country in 1848 and 1849.

As for the whaling village of **San Simeon** that grew up on what had been Pico's property, little is left today. In its heyday it boasted approximately 45 buildings. Perhaps the most important was the general store. Built in the 1850s, it was patronized by the whalers and their families, as well as the people on the nearby ranchos. Even though the village's buildings were lost to neglect and fires over the years, the general store survived. Eventually it was moved on horse-drawn skids to a site closer to the inland side of the bay. It is there to this day, and, believe it or not, it is *still* a general store!

The coming of the Hearst family changed the course of history for the San Simeon area. As I mentioned in the text, **George Hearst** didn't get *rich* in the gold fields, but he did take some of his Gold Country earnings to Nevada, where he invested in the silver mines of the newly discovered Comstock Lode. It was that investment that was the start of the Hearst fortune. So, in a roundabout way, the Gold Rush did play a part in George Hearst's rise to wealth and fame. Apart from his many mining ventures, Hearst went on to become a United States Senator and the owner of the San Francisco *Examiner* newspaper.

In addition to Rancho Piedra Blanca, the property acquired by Hearst included two smaller grants along the San Luis Obispo County coast. Rancho San Simeon (not to be confused with the village of the same name) was first granted to Jose Ramon Estrada in 1842. Sources disagree about the size of the original grant, with estimates ranging from 4,438 to 4,469 acres. The name honors Saint Simon (also spelled Simeon). Rancho Santa Rosa, which was first granted to Julian Estrada in 1841, consisted of approximately 13,184 acres. The name of this property is said to honor Saint Rosa de Lima (Rose of Lima), who for many years was the only female saint in the Americas.

When most Californians hear the name Hearst today, they probably think of **Hearst Castle.** The man who built it, **William Randolph Hearst,** became publisher of the *Examiner* at age 23 and went on to become a media magnate who owned a large chain of newspapers and many of the most popular magazines in America, along with movie companies, radio stations, and huge holdings of land in both the United States and Mexico. Hearst's fabulous lifestyle and career were one of the inspirations for Orson Welles' classic film *Citizen Kane* (in which the San Simeon estate became a huge and lonely palace called Xanadu).

With the building of Hearst Castle, San Simeon became a magnet for the rich and famous. In addition to numerous Hollywood celebrities, countless other notable people visited there. Among them were the great inventor Thomas Edison, President Calvin Coolidge, and Winston Churchill, the beloved statesman, writer, and prime minister of Great Britain.

The castle's architect is a fascinating person in her own right. **Julia Morgan** was the first woman to graduate from the University of California in civil engineering *and* the first woman to study architecture at the Ecole des Beaux-Arts (School of Fine Arts) in Paris. She created hundreds of private residences as well as a number of public buildings during her lifetime, but Hearst Castle remains her most famous achievement.

The donation of the castle to the State of California was made in the name of William Randolph Hearst's mother, Phoebe Apperson Hearst, who played an important part in influencing her son's interest in the art treasures of the old world. She was also a generous benefactor who had a special interest in education, archaeology, and anthropology. With her interest in art and education, it is only fitting that California's own castle, with all its antique treasures, was given to the people of the Golden State in her name.

ABOUT THE AUTHOR

Randall A. Reinstedt was born and raised on California's beautiful and historic Monterey Peninsula. After traveling widely throughout the world, he spent fifteen years teaching elementary school students, with special emphasis on California and local history. Today he continues to share his love of California's beauty and lore with young and old alike through his immensely popular publications. Among his many books is **More Than Memories: History & Happenings of the Monterey Peninsula,** an acclaimed history text for fourth-graders that is used in schools throughout the Monterey area.

Randy lives with his wife, Debbie, in a house overlooking the Pacific Ocean. In addition to his writing projects, he is in great demand as a lecturer on regional history to school and adult groups, and he frequently gives workshops for teachers on making history come alive in the classroom.

ABOUT THE ILLUSTRATOR

A native Californian, Ed Greco has spent most of his professional career as a graphic designer and illustrator. Born and raised in the Santa Clara Valley, Ed grew up studying and illustrating northern California, its environment, and its history.

Randall A. Reinstedt's
History & Happenings of California Series

Through colorful tales drawn from the rich store of California lore, this series introduces young readers to the historical heritage of California and the West. "Author's Notes" at the end of each volume provide information about the people, places, and events encountered in the text. Whether read for enjoyment or for learning, the books in this series bring the drama and adventure of yesterday to the young people of today.

Currently available in both hardcover and softcover:

Lean John, California's Horseback Hero

One-Eyed Charley, the California Whip

Otters, Octopuses, and Odd Creatures of the Deep

Stagecoach Santa

The Strange Case of the Ghosts of the Robert Louis Stevenson House

Tales and Treasures of California's Missions

Tales and Treasures of California's Ranchos

Tales and Treasures of the California Gold Rush

Hands-On History teacher resource books are available to accompany titles in the **History & Happenings of California Series.** Packed with projects and activities integrating skills across the curriculum, these imaginative resource books help bring California history to life in the classroom.

*For information about the **History & Happenings of California Series,** as well as other titles by Randy Reinstedt for both children and adults, please write:*

GHOST TOWN PUBLICATIONS
P. O. Drawer 5998
Carmel, CA 93921